...d
...s,
...l.

...r
...s

...experience and a passion for travel.

Rely on Thomas Cook as your travelling companion on your next trip and benefit from our unique heritage.

Thomas Cook **pocket** guides

CARDIFF

Written by Kerry Walker and updated by Victoria Trott

Published by Thomas Cook Publishing
A division of Thomas Cook Tour Operations Limited
Company registration no. 3772199 England
The Thomas Cook Business Park, Unit 9, Coningsby Road,
Peterborough PE3 8SB, United Kingdom
Email: books@thomascook.com, Tel: + 44 (0) 1733 416477
www.thomascookpublishing.com

Produced by Cambridge Publishing Management Limited
Burr Elm Court, Main Street, Caldecote CB23 7NU
www.cambridgepm.co.uk

ISBN: 978-1-84848-351-4

© 2006, 2008 Thomas Cook Publishing
This third edition © 2011
Text © Thomas Cook Publishing
Maps © Thomas Cook Publishing/PCGraphics (UK) Limited
Contains Ordnance Survey data © Crown copyright and database right 2010
Transport map © Communicarta Limited

Series Editor: Karen Beaulah
Production/DTP: Steven Collins

Printed and bound in Spain by GraphyCems

Cover photography © Camera Lucida/Alamy

CONTENTS

SYMBOLS KEY

The following symbols are used throughout this book:

ⓐ address ☎ telephone ⓦ website address
🕐 opening times ❶ important

The following symbols are used on the maps:

𝒊	information office	▨	point of interest
✈	airport	◯	city
✚	hospital	○	large town
🛡	police station	○	small town
🚌	bus station	═	motorway
🚆	railway station	━	main road
✝	cathedral	—	minor road
❶	numbers denote featured	—	railway
	cafés & restaurants	----	path

Hotels and restaurants are graded by approximate price as follows:
£ budget price **££** mid-range price **£££** expensive

▶ *The Pierhead and Millennium Centre as seen from Cardiff Bay*

INTRODUCING
Cardiff

Introduction

Europe's cultural Cinderella, Cardiff has brushed aside its industrial image and is looking better than ever. A multi-million-pound makeover has transformed the city in recent years, so if you haven't been for a while, you're in for a surprise. A glance at the glittering waterfront development of Cardiff Bay, the mighty Millennium Stadium, the iconic Senedd (National Assembly for Wales) and the new £675-million St David's shopping centre confirms that the Welsh capital has widely embraced change. The intoxicating result is what happens when 2,000 years of history meets the modern world.

With a population of just 325,000, Cardiff is a compact capital by international standards, but it outgrew its small-city boots long ago. The city is remarkably diverse, with world-class sights and late nights to rival those of any big city. Top that off with friendly locals, plentiful parks, elegant shopping arcades and lofty castles. Whether you're seeking Monet or Mozart, olde-worlde pubs or funky clubs, backpacker digs or chic boutique hotels, you're in the right place.

It isn't hard to see what makes the Welsh capital tick: rugby and real ale, comedy and culture, edgy art and avant-garde architecture all add to the appeal of this multifaceted city. Cardiff is a successful blend of the very old and the very new. Experience the best of both by climbing Cardiff Castle's Norman keep in the morning and sipping a latte in a glass-fronted café in Cardiff Bay in the afternoon, or by wallowing in the civic grandeur of Cathays Park's Edwardian buildings and then taking a tour of the futuristic Millennium Stadium.

But the story doesn't end there. Cardiff is simply an introduction – a great introduction – to southern Wales. Scratch beneath the surface to find surf, secluded coves and Celtic castles on the

Glamorgan Heritage Coast. Alternatively, venture further west
to the Gower Peninsula for prehistoric caves, standing stones and
clean waters. To the north, wild moors and conical peaks make
the Brecon Beacons perfect hiking and mountain-biking terrain.
So, depending on how long you're planning to stay, you can cram
a fair bit of the coast and country into a city break to Cardiff.

▲ *A view over the city from Penarth Headland*

When to go

If you can handle the vicissitudes of the weather, any time's a great time to visit Cardiff. Whatever's going on meteorologically, you're sure to receive a warm welcome.

SEASONS & CLIMATE

It's no secret that the weather in Wales is fickle – and Cardiff is no exception. You may find yourself basking in brilliant sunshine one minute, then taking shelter from a heavy downpour the next. But even if the sun doesn't shine, there's no reason to let wet weather put a dampener on your stay. Come well prepared with plenty of layers and waterproofs, particularly if you're planning on hiking and biking the coast or mountains.

May to September is your best bet for fine, sunny weather, as temperatures usually hit the 20°Cs (70°Fs). This is the time when the city really comes to life, with open-air concerts, festivals and carnivals (see page 10). The warmest months are also great for exploring the secluded coves of the Glamorgan Heritage Coast and Gower Penisula (see pages 104 and 118), or heading north to climb the peaks of the Brecon Beacons (see page 132).

While Cardiff is at its wettest during the winter (November to February), temperatures hover around 5°C (41°F) and rarely drop below freezing. This is a good time to visit if you want to avoid the crowds and explore the sights in relative peace.

Spring is the season to glimpse gardens in bloom or enjoy long coastal walks as the days get longer and the weather milder. Expect temperatures of approximately 10–15°C (50–60°F) from March to May, and a mixed bag of bright sunshine and blustery showers.

ANNUAL EVENTS

February & March

Six Nations Rugby Europe's leading teams battle it out for the title at the RBS Six Nations Championship, a highlight in the Rugby Union calendar. If you want a piece of the action, you should book tickets well in advance. The event takes place at Cardiff's Millennium Stadium (see page 66). Ⓦ www.rbs6nations.com

🔺 *Italy v Wales in the Six Nations Rugby Championship*

February–May

Artes Mundi Prize Artists from around the world compete for the coveted Artes Mundi Prize. Held every second year (even years), the contemporary visual arts competition pushes the creative boundaries at the National Museum Cardiff (see page 96) in the city centre. ☎ (029) 2055 5300 ⓦ www.artesmundi.org

July & August

Welsh Proms St David's Hall (see page 66) stages the Welsh Proms, a superb programme of orchestral and jazz highlights. From Brahms to Beethoven, these concerts are a must for classical music enthusiasts. ⓦ www.welshproms.co.uk

Cardiff Festival This must-see festival takes over Cardiff for two months of open-air concerts, theatre, live music, children's entertainment and funfairs (see page 12).

Admiral Cardiff Big Weekend The UK's biggest free outdoor party, the Admiral Cardiff Big Weekend is the grand finale to the summer festival. Live music, fairs and fireworks draw revellers to the city centre in droves (see page 13).

September

Cardiff Mardi Gras This mammoth Mardi Gras is free and takes place in Coopers Field. Thousands flock to Cardiff to celebrate the largest gay party in Wales, featuring top performers, fairground rides and market areas. ⓦ www.cardiffmardigras.co.uk

Great British Cheese Festival Join foodies from around the world at Britain's biggest cheese festival held in the lovely grounds of Cardiff Castle. More than 400 varieties to try. ☎ (029) 2023 0130 ⓦ www.thecheeseweb.com

October
Cardiff Half Marathon Feet pound Cardiff's streets as the annual half marathon comes to town. The race kicks off in Westgate Street and continues to Cardiff Bay and Canton, before returning to the finishing post at the Millennium Stadium (see page 66).
❶ 0845 308 4001 Ⓦ www.cardiffmarathon.org

November & December
Winter Wonderland 'Tis the season to get your skates on, as the gardens in front of City Hall (see page 92) are transformed into an ice rink. Warm up on the heated terrace, enjoy live music or test out the rides at the funfair. ❶ (029) 2023 0130
Ⓦ www.cardiffswinterwonderland.com
Wales Rally GB Cardiff steps up a gear for the finale of the 16-round FIA World Rally Championship (WRC). ❶ 0844 847 2251
Ⓦ www.walesrallygb.com

PUBLIC HOLIDAYS
New Year's Day 1 Jan
Good Friday 22 Apr 2011; 6 Apr 2012
Easter Monday 25 Apr 2011; 9 Apr 2012
May Day Bank Holiday 2 May 2011; 7 May 2012
Spring Bank Holiday 30 May 2011; 4 June 2012
Summer Bank Holiday 29 Aug 2011; 27 Aug 2012
Christmas Day 25 Dec
Boxing Day 26 Dec

Cardiff Festival

Summer in the Welsh capital spells the Cardiff Festival, a head-spinning mix of late-night parties, live concerts, classical highlights and family events. Headlining the city's summer calendar, this five-week open-air bash in July and August is one of the biggest in the UK. Expect an electric vibe, a fun-loving crowd and an eclectic programme stretching from improvised theatre to funfairs. Street entertainment and one-off performances are other big draws. The sheer size of the festival means it is split into a number of smaller events, many of which are free.

All the world's a stage at the **St Fagans National History Museum** (ⓐ St Fagans ⓣ (029) 2057 3500 ⓦ www.museumwales.ac.uk). Come here to see thespians take the stage by storm at the **Everyman Summer Theatre Festival** (ⓣ 0844 8700 887 ⓦ www.everymanfestival.co.uk), providing Shakespearean classics alongside children's favourites.

How can you keep the children amused? Take them to the Red Dragon Centre Family Festival, where they'll enjoy a carnival theatre show, or to the Grand Medieval Melee for a bout of archery or sword fighting. Classical music lovers can hear symphony orchestras, soloists and choirs hit the high notes at the Welsh Proms, held at St David's Hall (see page 66). The Hall also hosts Cardiff Comedy Festival, which features some of the UK's top comedians over ten days.

Foodies should make a beeline for Cardiff Bay's International Food & Drink Festival, whetting appetites with flavours from France, Germany, Italy and Spain, as well as traditional Welsh fare. Over Summer Bank Holiday, the bay is the location of lots of nautical fun during Cardiff Harbour Festival.

Flamboyant parades, the sound of steel drums and samba music round out the festival in style, as the multicultural MAS Carnival comes to town. This builds up to the grand finale: the three-day Admiral Cardiff Big Weekend, featuring live music, a huge funfair and fireworks each night. With a line-up like this, it's no surprise that people come back year after year.

For more information, contact ☎ (029) 2087 2087
Ⓦ www.cardiff-festival.com

🔺 *Family fun – with lobsters – at Cardiff Festival*

History

Although Cardiff's roots can be traced back as far as 600 BC when the Celts invaded Europe, the city was first established when the Romans built a fort here in AD 55. This is the site where Cardiff Castle now stands, sheltering over 2,000 years of Welsh history.

Following centuries of Viking, Norman and Irish invasions, a key turning point in Cardiff's history took place in the 16th century. In 1542 Thomas Capper was burnt at the stake for heresy and was subsequently hailed Wales's first religious martyr. That same year the second Act of Union was introduced, which divided Wales into shires, established a new justice system and made English the official language. From then on, Welsh speakers were banned from holding public office. This bone of contention sparked an age-old conflict between England and Wales that still bubbles under the surface today.

In 1648 Cardiff was back on the map when Welsh participation in the English Civil War culminated in the bloody Battle of St Fagans. To this day, battle re-enactments take place at St Fagans National History Museum (see page 18), where these historic events unfolded.

THE WELSH NOT
The Welsh language is an integral part of Cardiff's identity, so it's hard to believe that little more than 150 years ago people were punished for uttering a single word in Welsh. At school children were forced to speak English, and those who dared to converse in Welsh were beaten or forced to wear the loathed 'Welsh Not', a wooden necklace that was a mark of shame.

Cardiff prospered, industry flourished and the population spiralled during the 19th century, when the Marquis of Bute opened Cardiff's first dock in 1839 and the first rail line was built in 1845, linking Cardiff to nearby coal-producing valleys.

The wealth that coal mining and iron smelting brought during the Industrial Revolution meant that Cardiff grew steadily. It was finally granted city status in 1905, and was famous at that time as the world's biggest coal exporter.

The coal industry gradually declined and the face of the city changed – Welsh was made the official language in 1942 and Cardiff became the capital of Wales in 1955. This vibrant university city has successfully propelled itself into the 21st century, boasting the stunning new waterfront development of Cardiff Bay (see page 76) and more parks per square mile than any other UK city. In 2009 Cardiff confirmed its status as one of the UK's major shopping destinations with the opening of the new St David's 2 centre.

◔ A statue in Cardiff Bay recalls the city's proud mining heritage

Lifestyle

Modern and buzzing, Cardiff has 26,000 students, making it one of Europe's youngest capitals. Perhaps the real secret of this Welsh beauty lies in its scale – small enough to get around easily, yet big enough to feel like a city. Or maybe it's because Cardiff remains rooted in its heritage, despite the multi-million-pound regeneration projects that have revamped the city.

Many people born and bred in Cardiff and the surrounding area are irrefutably Welsh and proud of it, showing growing confidence and a strong sense of national identity. While the vast majority speak English as their first language, they often don't like to be called British, or, worse still, English. Impress the locals by dropping a few words of Welsh into the conversation. Although Cardiff has been anglicised, more people still speak Welsh than any other surviving Celtic tongue.

Down to earth and friendly, the locals are a charismatic bunch who like to sing (as the city's high proportion of choirs shows) and love to laugh. Cardiff is, in fact, the UK's comedy capital. Witticisms, quips and banter always go down well with a pint of locally brewed Brains bitter.

Aware of their tradition but by no means traditional, Cardiff's residents are a young, party-loving lot that like to play as hard as they work, as a night out in the trendy bars along Cardiff Bay (see page 87) or in the city centre's lively pubs and clubs confirms.

While song and laughter are close to Cardiff's heart, the capital has only one true passion: rugby. Love it or loathe it, the locals live and breathe this rough and rugged sport, with local team the **Cardiff Blues** (❶ 0845 345 1400 ⓦ www.cardiffblues.com) enjoying a huge following. Join the fans to soak up the atmosphere in their new stadium, which is also home to Cardiff City FC.

⬥ *Two Cardiff favourites – Brains beer and Welsh rugby union*

Culture

Sassy, bold and ever-evolving, today's Cardiff has got cultural clout, rising out of the industrial ashes as a multicultural and multilingual city. With a thriving arts and music scene, the city is currently making waves with edgy art galleries, world-class auditoriums and well-preserved Victorian buildings. These qualities helped the city make the shortlist for the 2008 European Capital of Culture.

Whether you prefer opera greats or pints down the local, Cardiff hits the spot. A thriving student population and pioneering urban regeneration projects like Cardiff Bay (see page 76) have made the jewel in the Welsh crown glitter once again. From strings and sopranos at St David's Hall (see page 66) to Impressionist watercolours at the National Museum Cardiff (see page 96), Cardiff is a magnet to culture vultures.

The first stop for music lovers should be St David's Hall, a 2,000-seat venue offering some of the best acoustics in Europe, which hosts the Welsh Proms in summer and the biennial Cardiff Singer of the World Competition. Another must is the glittering slate-and-glass Wales Millennium Centre in Cardiff Bay (see page 83), where the Welsh National Opera performs. This is also the place to catch everything from West End musicals to rock concerts.

Avid theatregoers should book tickets for the turn-of-the-century New Theatre (see page 96), one of Wales's leading performing arts venues that welcomes big names to the stage, including the Royal National Theatre. For quirky adaptations, try the Sherman Theatre (see page 96). Chapter Arts Centre (see page 65) presents thought-provoking productions in one of Europe's largest cultural venues.

Six km (4 miles) west of Cardiff, the open-air **St Fagans National History Museum** (🕐 (029) 2057 3500 🌐 www.museumwales.ac.uk)

The Wales Millennium Centre is the home of the Welsh National Opera

explores 500 years of Welsh history and heritage in the 40-hectare (100-acre) grounds of 16th-century St Fagans Castle. Displays and craft workshops are held in 40 traditional buildings, including a school, chapel and Workmen's Institute. Step inside to see the galleries exhibiting Welsh costume and farming implements. Native breeds of livestock roam the paddocks and farmyards, and demonstrations of traditional farming tasks take place daily. If you're into art, get your fix for free at National Museum Cardiff (see page 96), showcasing the biggest collection of French Impressionist paintings outside of Paris. Works on display also range from old masters like Rubens and Van Dyck to contemporary sculpture.

Off the beaten tourist track, the capital is punctuated with smaller, more intimate galleries. Make for the **Albany Gallery** (ⓐ 74b Albany Road ⓣ (029) 2048 7158 ⓦ www.albanygallery.com) and **Martin Tinney Gallery** (ⓐ 18 St Andrew's Crescent ⓣ (029) 2064 1411 ⓦ www.artwales.com) to enjoy a taste of modern Welsh art.

With culture at its core, it's little wonder that Cardiff has given rise to some of the music, literary and art worlds' biggest names. Among them are Shirley Bassey, who was born here, the singer Charlotte Church, best-selling authors Roald Dahl and Ken Follett, actor Griff Rhys Jones, and bands the Manic Street Preachers and Super Furry Animals. The city that inspired these stars beckons.

⊙ *The restaurants and bars of Mill Lane*

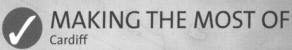

MAKING THE MOST OF
Cardiff

Shopping

Whether you're seeking funky designer labels or antique shops, markets with local flavour or big high-street names, Cardiff comes up with the goods. Most shops cluster around central St Mary Street, High Street, Castle Street, Duke Street and Queen Street. The city centre is liberally criss-crossed with pedestrianised Victorian arcades, housing everything from one-off boutiques to bookshops and laid-back cafés, where you can rest your feet after a morning's shop. For the latest trends, make for the split-level **Queens Arcade Shopping Centre** (**①** (029) 2022 3581 **Ⓦ** www.queensarcade.info). Home to chains like **Debenhams** (**①** 0844 561 6161), **M&S** (**①** (029) 2037 8211) and **BHS** (**①** (029) 2039 0167), St David's shopping centre on Queen Street (see page 70) is a good choice if it rains or you want to shop under one roof. Its neighbour and (bigger) little brother, **St David's 2** (**①** 0800 345 7547 **Ⓦ** www.stdavids2.com), opened in 2009 and is home to the largest John Lewis store outside London (**①** (029) 2053 6000 **Ⓦ** www.johnlewis.com). The glass-fronted **Capitol Shopping Centre** (**ⓐ** Queen St **①** (029) 2022 3683 **Ⓦ** www.capitol-shopping-centre.co.uk) hosts high-street names like **H&M** (**①** (029) 2072 7950) and **Kookai** (**①** (029) 2039 5080).

Crammed with fresh produce from creamy Welsh cheeses to organic coffee, Cardiff's Victorian **Central Market** (**ⓐ** St Mary St **①** (029) 2087 1214 **Ⓦ** www.cardiff-market.co.uk) opens from 08.00 to 17.30 Monday to Saturday. You'll also find second-hand books, specialist records, jewellery, local crafts and leather goods. On Sunday morning sniff out local specialities such as hot Welsh cakes, honey and organic lamb at the Riverside Market (see page 69) opposite the Millennium Stadium.

🔺 *The elegant split-level Castle Arcade*

Eating & drinking

Once upon a time Cardiff's culinary endeavours may have been limited to laverbread (see page 26), leeks and Welsh lamb. But those days are long gone, as the forward-thinking, multi-ethnic capital moves into new gastro waters. OK, so you'll still find Welsh staples on the menu if you want them, but with a modern twist and an emphasis on organic, locally sourced produce.

World flavours also make an appearance, with a mind-boggling array of restaurants, bistros and cafés serving everything from 5-star French cuisine to fiery Bengali curries and sushi on a conveyor belt. So, whether your idea of heaven is a spicy samosa in a central curry house or fresh fish in Cardiff Bay's seafood restaurants, you won't go hungry here. The good news is that eating out is still affordable compared to other big cities – pleasing for the stomach and the pocket!

You can pretty much eat your way around the world in Cardiff. For brilliant baltis and cheap-and-cheerful Chinese or Indian buffets, make a beeline for Albany Road, City Road and Clifton Street in Roath, one of the capital's main student districts. In the city centre and Cathays, you'll find everything from Thai restaurants and Greek tavernas to trendy New York-style delis and Japanese noodle bars. Hungry students and clubbers find late-night, post-party food in

PRICE CATEGORIES

The restaurant price guides used in this book indicate the approximate cost of a three-course meal for one person, excluding drinks, at the time of writing.

£ under £20   ££ £20–35   £££ over £35

City Road, Albany Road, Whitchurch Road and High Street. The fast-food outlets here selling burgers, kebabs, pizzas, standard Chinese fare and fish 'n' chips might not exactly be gourmet, but they serve their purpose with cheap and filling food. Mingle with Cardiff's hip crowd on the buzzing waterfront, the place to come for the freshest seafood and sweeping views. Around Mermaid Quay smart restaurants, trendy fish restaurants, Italian trattorias and bars all jostle for your attention. In summer it's a great spot for alfresco dining on the terrace.

Every Sunday the Riverside Market (see page 69) tempts foodies with a mouth-watering selection of fresh, local produce. The perfect pre-picnic shop, here you can fill your bags with Gower cockles, Caerphilly cheese, laverbread and creamy Welsh fudge. It's best to arrive before 13.00, when the stalls start to sell out. From Monday

⬤ *You'll find plenty of fresh fish and seafood in Cardiff's restaurants*

LEARNING TO LOVE LAVER

Traditionally served with cockles and bacon, laverbread (or *bara lawr*) is a staple of the hearty Welsh breakfast. To make the 'bread', seaweed is boiled for several hours to make a soft paste, which is then rolled in oatmeal and fried. Edible seaweed may not seem all that appetising, but most locals beg to differ. Hence the fact that this pungent, nutritious speciality appears on many menus.

⬥ *Traditional Welsh breakfast – laverbread*

to Saturday, Cardiff's Central Market (see page 22) has a selection of organic fruit and vegetables, Welsh cheeses, seafood, fresh bread and cakes.

Cardiff has plenty of parks and gardens where, weather permitting, you can enjoy a leisurely picnic. Lay your blanket by the lake in leafy Roath Park (see page 62) and tuck into Welsh specialities. Another popular choice is centrally located Bute Park (see page 60), where picnickers can laze by the River Taff's banks. A few miles out of town, the Edwardian Dyffryn Gardens (see page 106) is a lovely spot for a picnic on a summer's day. Further afield, the Glamorgan Heritage Coast (see page 104) and Gower's secluded bays (see page 118) are ideal if you're seeking gorgeous views and perfect peace.

When it comes to the local specialities, Cardiff whets appetites with wholesome, hearty dishes using tasty, simple ingredients. Savour specialities like Welsh rarebit (cheese on toast made with ale), laverbread (see opposite), tender Welsh lamb and fruity *bara brith* tea loaf. Warming on those damp, dreary days are *crempog* (pancakes with salty Welsh butter) and *cawl* (a filling stew made with bacon, mutton and leeks). There are some flavoursome local cheeses to try, including soft Abergavenny goat's cheese, pungent Granston Blue and tangy Caerphilly. Cardiff's proximity to the coast means that fresh seafood is a staple, with restaurants serving everything from cockles to beer-battered cod.

The tipple of choice in Cardiff is beer, particularly the locally brewed Brains varieties. Head to one of the city's many pubs to drink pints of amber-coloured Brains Bitter with a sweet-malt flavour, Brains Dark ale or hoppy Brains SA with a bitter-sweet finish and fruit note. Nearby vineyards also produce wines and grape-based spirits. Refreshing alternatives are hand-pressed cider, elderflower drinks and perry (a fermented pear beverage).

Entertainment & nightlife

Home to some of the UK's leading performing-arts venues, more pubs and clubs than you can shake a stick at, plus a student population that just wants to have fun, Cardiff rocks by night. Moving from pints in a friendly watering hole in Cathays (see page 100) to cocktails in the chic bars dotting Cardiff Bay (see page 87) and late-night clubbing in the city centre, you're practically guaranteed a good night out here.

Locals tend to hit the pubs and bars early (around 20.00). Although the UK introduced 24-hour drinking laws in 2005, punters still have to drink up by 23.00 in many of the smaller pubs in Cardiff's residential areas and outskirts. Central pubs tend to stay open slightly later, while the majority of clubs pump out tunes until around 03.00 at weekends.

Culture vultures are well catered for with a plethora of theatres, concert halls and cinemas – from strings and sopranos at St David's Hall (see page 66) to ballet and opera at the Wales Millennium Centre (see page 83). If you want to book tickets for a performance, you'll often get the best deal by contacting the venue direct. Alternatively, **Ticket Line** (ⓐ 47 Westgate St ⓣ (029) 2023 0130 ⓦ www.ticketlineuk.com) sells tickets for concerts, sporting events and musicals.

Wall-to-wall pubs and bars vie for custom in central Cardiff, around St Mary Street and Mill Lane. A mixture of spit-and-sawdust pubs, trendy bars and everything in between, this is the place to come if you like your music loud, crowd young and vibe buzzing. Cathays pulls the crowds with a cocktail of funky bars, laid-back pubs and relaxed beer gardens.

A relative newcomer to the Welsh capital's nightlife scene is Cardiff Bay, with a string of sleek bars overlooking the illuminated

● *A hot summer's night at the Terra Nova bar (see page 88)*

🔵 *St David's Hall is the place to go for serious music lovers*

WHAT'S ON?

These two websites are very useful for planning culture,
cackles and quaffing in Cardiff. They feature information
about entertainment and nightlife, plus up-to-date listings
of events taking place in the city:

Cardiff What's On Find out what's on during your stay
with this online listing of the arts, cinema, comedy, music,
theatre and clubs. The site is updated daily.
Ⓦ www.walesonline.co.uk/cardiffwhatson

View Cardiff A comprehensive online guide to gigs, theatre,
comedy and film screenings. Ⓦ www.viewcardiff.co.uk

waterfront. Wood floors, floor-to-ceiling glass and minimalist chic
set the scene, but there's nothing minimalist about the fun to be
had here. Vast amounts of money have been poured into this area's
regeneration, and the entertainment on offer is varied, stretching
from live music to comedy.

Night owls should head for the clubs in central Cardiff to dance
till the wee hours. St Mary Street is a safe bet for after-dark fun.

Performing-arts culture comes in high doses in Cardiff.
Complementing what's on offer at the Wales Millennium Centre,
St David's Hall (see page 66) is a must for serious music buffs.

If theatre appeals, the Sherman Theatre (see page 96) and
Chapter Arts Centre (see page 65) beckon; the latter also shows
art-house and foreign-language films (most with English subtitles).
Blockbuster movies grace the 12 giant screens at the Odeon Cinema
in the Red Dragon Centre (see page 149), while comedy fans should
head to the Glee Club (Ⓣ 0871 472 0400 Ⓦ www.glee.co.uk).

Sport & relaxation

SPECTATOR SPORTS

If the locals aren't practising on the pitch, you'll find them cheering on their team down the pub. The three big spectator sports are rugby, football and cricket. The first two are played at Cardiff City Stadium (ⓦ www.cardiffcitystadium.co.uk), home to Cardiff Blues RFC (see page 16) and Cardiff City FC (ⓣ 0845 345 1400 ⓦ www.cardiffcityfc.co.uk), while cricket is purveyed by Glamorgan County Cricket Club at the **SWALEC Stadium** (ⓐ Sophia Gardens, Cathedral Road ⓣ 0871 282 3401 ⓦ www.glamorgancricket.com). The **Millennium Stadium** (see page 66) hosts the major sporting events.

PARTICIPATION SPORTS

Hiking Wales is made for walking, so bring some sturdy boots and tackle the coastal paths spanning the Glamorgan Heritage Coast and the Gower Peninsula (see pages 104 and 118). Serious trekkers take on the 89-km (55-mile) Taff Trail (see page 137).

Swimming You'd have to be brave to take a dip out of season in the Bristol Channel but Cardiff has plenty of indoor options such as the **Eastern Leisure Centre** (ⓐ Llanrumney Av, Llanrumney ⓣ (029) 2079 6616), with a pool, gym and sauna. The city's jewel is the Olympic-quality pool at the Cardiff International Sports Village (see page 84).

Watersports Surfing and kite-surfing are all the rage on the Glamorgan Heritage Coast (see page 112). Some of the best waves hit the beaches of Porthcawl and Dunraven Bay near

Southerndown. Further west on the Gower Peninsula, adrenalin junkies test out everything from skiing and wakeboarding to kayaking and coasteering.

RELAXATION

If you want to splash out on the ultimate spa experience, there's only one place to do it. The Marine Spa in the St David's Hotel (see page 37) offers an arm-long list of therapies. Beauty comes at a cost, but the views of Cardiff Bay from the relaxation lounge are simply priceless.

● *Hikers on the Taff Trail in the Brecon Beacons*

Accommodation

From chic boutique suites to country retreats, and cheap digs to spa hotels, Cardiff offers a mind-boggling array of accommodation to suit every pocket. If you're on a tight budget, there are a number of decent hostels and guesthouses just a short bus ride away from the centre; many include breakfast in the room rate. If money is no object, splash out on a grand Victorian hotel in the city centre to be at the heart of the action, or choose a contemporary suite with a view of Cardiff Bay.

HOTELS

The Big Sleep Hotel ££ Looking for a room with a view? This place is for you. With its funky, retro design, this ultra-cool hotel is one of Cardiff's tallest, affording sweeping views over the city and bay. Glam yet affordable, the converted 1960s block offers sleek rooms and efficient service. ❸ Bute Terrace ❶ (029) 2063 6363 Ⓦ www.thebigsleephotel.com

Preste Gaarden Hotel ££ Once a vicarage and home to the Norwegian Consulate, this Victorian town house is exceptionally pretty (inside and out) and fully deserves its three-star status. ❸ 181 Cathedral Road ❶ (029) 2022 8607 Ⓦ www.cosycardiffhotel.co.uk

PRICE CATEGORIES

The ratings below indicate the approximate cost of a room for two people for one night, excluding breakfast.

£ under £40 ££ £40–70 £££ over £70

Sandringham Hotel ££ Family-run traditional hotel on the city's main street. There's a ground-floor café, which has live jazz on Monday to Friday evenings. It's a short walk to all the main sights. ⓐ 21 St Mary St ⓣ (029) 2023 2161 ⓦ www.sandringham-hotel.com

Sleeperz Hotel ££ A stylish budget hotel next to the bus and train stations, so ideal for late arrivals or early starters. Rooms are small

🔺 *Great views and retro styling at The Big Sleep Hotel*

but there's free Wi-Fi and free calls to UK landlines.
Ⓐ Station Approach, Saunders Road Ⓣ (029) 2047 8747
Ⓦ www.sleeperz.com

Barcelo-Cardiff Angel Hotel £££ Very posh. Rooms don't come cheap, but if polished marble floors, sweeping staircases and crystal chandeliers are your idea of the basics, you're in the right place. On Cardiff Castle's doorstep, the hotel has Wi-Fi and 24-hour room service. Ⓐ Castle St Ⓣ 0800 652 8413 Ⓦ www.barcelo-hotels.co.uk

Jolyons Boutique Hotel £££ Opposite the Wales Millennium Centre, this intimate boutique hotel has six sumptuous rooms. Sink into your king-sized bed, or choose a room with a whirlpool and views of Cardiff Bay. Relax with a coffee by the wood-burning stove in the contemporary bar. Ⓐ 5 Bute Crescent Ⓣ (029) 2048 8775
Ⓦ www.jolyons.co.uk

Lincoln House Hotel £££ A small, stylish hotel in a Victorian town house in Cardiff's most fashionable area. Facilities include free Wi-Fi and parking; the penthouse suite has two bedrooms and a kitchen.
Ⓐ 118–120 Cathedral Road Ⓣ (029) 2039 5558
Ⓦ www.lincolnhotel.co.uk

Old Post Office £££ Dine and sleep in style at this contemporary hotel in St Fagans. Light-filled rooms offer simple sophistication, clean contours and plump beds. Foodies flock to the restaurant where award-winning chef Wesley Hammond cooks up a storm. Ⓐ Greenwood Lane Ⓣ (029) 2056 5400
Ⓦ www.theoldpostofficerestaurant.co.uk

St David's Hotel & Spa £££ The town's most talked about hotel needs little introduction. Guests can enjoy views of Cardiff Bay from their private balconies, dine in the award-winning Tempus bar and restaurant and relax in the hydrotherapy spa. It might be pricey, but it's pure, unashamed indulgence. ⓐ Havannah St ⓣ (029) 2045 4045 ⓦ www.thestdavidshotel.com

⬥ *Top-of-the-range accommodation at St David's Hotel & Spa*

BED & BREAKFAST

Acorn Lodge £ A good cheapie, this intimate B&B is bright and clean. Cosy rooms have a TV and tea-making facilities, and the friendly owners are more than happy to help. A 15-minute walk from the centre, the small guesthouse has a pretty garden and the breakfast comes recommended. ⓐ 182 Cathedral Road ⓣ (029) 2022 1373

Austin's £ The rooms won't win any design awards, but they are spotless. This little red-brick guesthouse overlooks the River Taff and is just a few steps from the castle. Awarded 2 stars by the Wales Tourist Board, it's basic but good value. ⓐ 11 Coldstream Terrace ⓣ (029) 2037 7148 ⓦ www.hotelcardiff.com

Beaufort Guest House £££ This high-ceilinged Victorian town house has elegant en-suite rooms in creams and blues. Expect a warm welcome and delicious Welsh breakfast. ⓐ 65 Cathedral Road ⓣ (029) 2023 7003 ⓦ www.beauforthousecardiff.co.uk

Gelynis Farm and Guest House £££ This 16th-century stone cottage in the heart of green countryside is just 8 km (5 miles) from Cardiff (a ten-minute train ride). Near Castell Coch, the farmhouse has its own fruit farm and is a great base for those who want to walk the Taff Trail. ⓐ Morganstown ⓣ (029) 2084 4440 ⓦ www.gelynisfarm.co.uk

The Laurels £££ A real find is this dreamy, whitewashed cottage in St Fagans. With easy access to the M4, this low-key, family-run hotel offers cosy rooms and has village charm. Buses run frequently to the city centre. ⓐ 1 The Laurels, Cardiff Road ⓣ (029) 2056 6668 ⓦ www.beechwoodonline.co.uk

HOSTELS

Cardiff Backpacker Hostel £ The best budget deal in town is this central, laid-back hostel. A five-minute walk from the station, dorms and private rooms are clean and bedding is provided. Facilities include Internet access, a communal kitchen and bar. A hearty Welsh breakfast is also included in the price – but you have to stay for a minimum of two nights. ⓐ 98 Neville St ⓣ (029) 2034 5577 ⓦ www.cardiffbackpacker.com

Nos da Inns @ The Riverbank £ The riverside relative of Cardiff Backpackers has been revamped as the Hilton of the hostel world. Backpackers and families can expect en-suite, no-frills rooms. There are left-luggage facilities, a 24-hour check-in, travel desk and nightclub. The barbecue area is popular in summer. ⓐ 53–59 Despenser St ⓣ (029) 2037 8866 ⓦ www.cardiffbackpacker.com

YHA Cardiff £ Cheap digs can be found at this attractive red-brick hostel near Roath Park. Dorms are basic but clean, and there's a lounge and kitchen for guest use. Internet access and lockers are available. Unless you're a YHA member, you'll have to pay a surcharge. ⓐ 2 Wedal Road ⓣ 0845 371 9311 ⓦ www.yha.org.uk

CAMPSITES

Cardiff Caravan Park at Pontcanna Fields £ This small, well-kept site scores points for its central location. Bute Park is within arm's reach and the city centre is a 15-minute walk away. The 93 pitches are spacious, showers hot and facilities clean. Open year-round, the site has a laundry, resident warden and cycle hire. ⓐ Fields Park Road ⓣ (029) 2039 8362 ⓦ www.cardiff.gov.uk

THE BEST OF CARDIFF

Whether you're in Cardiff to do a quick bit of business or to enjoy a leisurely immersion in the city's cultural and natural delights, there are some sights and attractions that you simply mustn't miss.

TOP 10 ATTRACTIONS

- **Millennium Stadium** Massive sporting events raise pulses at this iconic landmark – the ultra-modern face of the new city (see page 66).

- **Cardiff Castle** Disney couldn't have done a better job with the turrets and towers of this picture-perfect castle in central Cardiff (see page 60).

- **Techniquest** Scintillating science is the focus of this hands-on discovery museum and planetarium in Cardiff Bay (see page 80).

- **National Museum Cardiff** This is the place to come if you want to admire Monets and van Goghs alongside Celtic coins and cannonballs (see page 96).

- **Llandaff Cathedral** Set in leafy Llandaff, this cathedral houses Sir Jacob Epstein's eye-catching *Christ in Majesty* statue (see page 62).

- **St David's Hall** High notes reverberate at the National Concert Hall of Wales, as world-class soloists and orchestras take the stage by storm (see page 66).

- **St Fagans National History Museum** Dip into the rich pot of Welsh history and heritage at this free open-air museum, set in the 40-hectare (100-acre) grounds of the 16th-century castle (see page 18).

- **Dyffryn Gardens** Cardiff and its surrounding districts have a few surprises up their green sleeves and this listed Edwardian garden is one of them (see page 106).

- **Senedd (National Assembly for Wales)** A marvel of modern art and energy efficiency, the National Assembly for Wales dominates Cardiff Bay with its smooth contours and wave-shaped roof (see page 79).

- **Roath Park** Pinned at the city's green heart, this park has kept its Victorian feel and is the perfect place to escape the crowds (see page 62).

◆ Treorchy Male Voice Choir

Suggested itineraries

HALF-DAY: CARDIFF IN A HURRY

Kick off your whirlwind stay in Cardiff Bay (see page 76), walking along the waterfront to spy the slate-and-steel Wales Millennium Centre (see page 83) and striking Senedd (see page 79), plus a string of contemporary sculptures. Following a quick caffeine fix at Mermaid Quay, hop aboard a Cardiff Cat (see page 78) to soak up more sights from the water and reach the city centre.

1 DAY: TIME TO SEE A LITTLE MORE

If you're staying the day, it would be rude not to take a peek behind Cardiff Castle's sturdy doors (see page 60) – climb the Norman keep for the best views. Nearby, take a behind-the-scenes tour of the iconic Millennium Stadium (see page 66) or speed shop in

○ *A tranquil view of Cardiff Bay*

Queens Arcade (see page 22). Nip into the indoor market and leave with a bag full of Welsh goodies.

2–3 DAYS: TIME TO SEE MUCH MORE

You've seen the stadium, climbed the castle and now you want more? Head to Cathays Park (see page 90), where fountains and marble statues glam up City Hall (see page 92). Next up is the National Museum Cardiff (see page 96), where you can wallow in art and Wales's natural history. Weather permitting, pack up a picnic and make for Roath Park (see page 62) to relax in the rose gardens, or central Bute Park (see page 60) to laze beside the snaking River Taff. An afternoon is also well spent exploring the open-air St Fagans National History Museum (see page 18). As night falls, see stars through glass windows in Mermaid Quay's avant-garde bars or on the stage at St David's Hall (see page 66).

Those with itchy feet can venture further afield to Llandaff Cathedral (see page 62), home to the controversial *Christ in Majesty* statue, or classic Welsh beauty Castell Coch (see page 137) tucked away in the hills – all silvery turrets, round towers and vaulted ceilings, it's classic fairy-tale stuff.

LONGER: ENJOYING CARDIFF TO THE FULL

Travellers with time on their hands can sample all Cardiff has to offer, and then some. Go west to kayak or kite-surf on the 23-km (14-mile) Glamorgan Heritage Coast (see page 104), studded with sheer cliffs and sheltered coves. The unspoilt Gower Peninsula (see page 118) hides secluded bays, caves and its fair share of fossils.

North of Cardiff, Caerphilly sits in the shadow of a castle with a leaning tower to rival Pisa's. Meanwhile, hikers don walking boots to scale the peaks of the Brecon Beacons (see page 132).

Something for nothing

The best things in Cardiff are free, so you'll be glad to know you don't have to splurge to enjoy all this city has to offer. Take in a free exhibition (or two) in the top museums and galleries, sculpture-hop your way along futuristic Cardiff Bay (see page 76), lose yourself in a warren of Victorian buildings in Cathays Park (see page 90), or simply chill in the capital's parks and gardens. Come in summer for a non-stop line-up of free concerts, parties and parades at the Cardiff Festival (see page 12).

It won't cost you a penny to catch one of the lunchtime, afternoon or early evening performances at the Wales Millennium Centre (see page 83). The iconic venue in Cardiff Bay stages everything from a cappella choirs to classical, jazz and world music. St David's Hall (see page 66) regularly stages free exhibitions, plus contemporary and traditional craft displays by some of Wales's finest makers and designers in the exhibition spaces.

One (free) bite isn't enough at the huge National Museum Cardiff (see page 96). The scope of its ambition makes it simply too toothsome: from geology to marine biodiversity and from art to archaeology, here you can marvel at Impressionist masterpieces and shipwrecks, or trace the country's geology back 700 million years. At St Fagans National History Museum (see page 18) you can discover Welsh history and heritage. If you don't have the time to tackle the Taff Trail (see page 137), the 8-km (5-mile) St Fagans Walk starts here. For something a touch gentler, a stroll in Roath Park (see page 62) blows away the cobwebs. There are rose and dahlia gardens, subtropical greenhouses, and wildfowl (including cormorants) roosting on the lake's islands. Trying to spot the lighthouse that pays tribute to Captain Scott may not be quite on a par with the latest computer games, but it's good, clean (and free) fun.

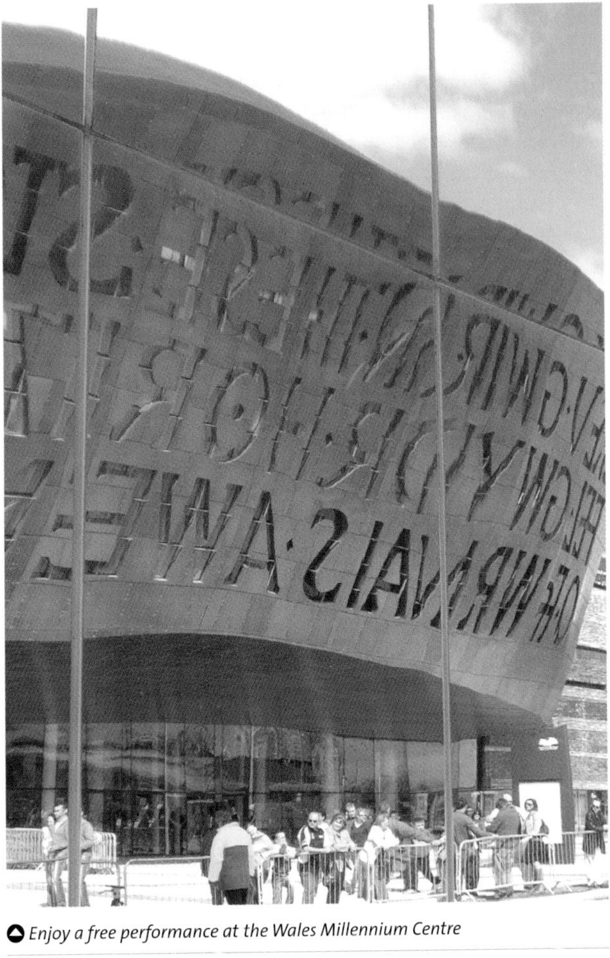

Enjoy a free performance at the Wales Millennium Centre

When it rains

The savvy locals have never let a bit of drizzle from the valleys get them down, so why should you? Cardiff cleverly compensates for Wales's heavy downpours and all-too-spontaneous showers with a host of undercover attractions.

The city's central labyrinth of Victorian arcades and crystalline shopping centres is a great place to take shelter, whether you're trying on the latest high-street trends in the Capitol Shopping Centre (see page 22), or nipping into the boutiques lining Queens Arcade (see page 22), where high-street shops mix with smart boutiques and speciality outlets. Cardiff's Central Market is indoors (see page 22), where you can soak up the lively atmosphere and sniff out local produce. Little wonder then that when Wales rains, Cardiff shops.

Discover Cardiff Bay's top indoor attractions, starting with Wales's political engine the Senedd (see page 79). Children in tow? Take them to Techniquest (see page 80), an interactive science museum where they can push, pull and prod to their heart's content.

If all that sightseeing has worked up an appetite, warm up with a latte and panini at Coffee Mania (see page 85). Cultural shelter is on offer at City Hall in Cathays Park (see page 92). Carved from white Portland stone, the impressive building houses Joseph Farquharson's winter art collection. The headline attraction, though, is the Marble Hall on the second floor, where marble statues of Welsh heroes like Boudicca and St David vie for your attention.

Nearby is the National Museum Cardiff (see page 96), where you can brush up against Impressionist masterpieces. Highlights include Monet's *Waterlilies* and a version of Rodin's famous bronze statue *The Kiss*. As well as art, the museum has intriguing displays on biodiversity, geology, archaeology and industry. The eclectic mix of permanent collections and cutting-edge exhibitions provides more than enough entertainment on a damp afternoon. The pub is a fine institution that relieves the dull patches of a Welsh winter: real ale on tap, squashy leather chairs and a roaring fire are the perfect antidotes to rainy weather.

🔺 Check out the local produce at the Central Market

On arrival

TIME DIFFERENCE

Cardiff's clocks follow Greenwich Mean Time (GMT). During Daylight Saving Time (end Mar–end Oct) the clocks are put forward one hour.

ARRIVING

By air

Many international airlines serve **Cardiff Airport** (ⓐ Rhoose ⓣ (01446) 711111 ⓦ www.tbicardiffairport.com), 19 km (12 miles) west of the city centre. Cardiff's compact and modern airport offers a range of facilities. You'll find free luggage trolleys and a tourist information centre in the arrivals hall, a bureau de change on the first floor and an ATM in the departure lounge. There is a food village where you can grab a snack on the run, plus a number of shops for last-minute gifts.

The airport has good public transport connections to the city centre. Trains run every hour between the airport and Cardiff Central Station, with onward connections to other destinations. Buy tickets on board the trains from Cardiff Airport or at the train station ticket desk at Cardiff Central Station. The **Airbus Xpress** (ⓦ www.cardiffbus.com) service X91 operates every two hours between Cardiff and the airport daily. A taxi from the airport to the city centre should cost around £26.

By rail

Trains pull into the heart of the city at **Cardiff Central Station**, Wales's largest railway station (ⓐ Central Square ⓣ 0845 6061 660). You'll find payphones, toilets and ATMs at the station. The concourse has a café, bookshop and newsagents stocking international press. You can book tickets in advance at the station or order them online. Travel is slightly cheaper off-peak (outside of rush hour Monday to Friday and at weekends).

By road

Cardiff's bus station, in Wood Street, is located close to Cardiff Central Station. National Express (see page 147) stops at rank A and serves destinations including London, Bristol, Oxford and Glasgow.

The M4 links Cardiff to other UK cities. From London, the motorway passes Bath and Bristol, before crossing the Severn Bridge, which connects England to Wales. Make sure you've got some spare change

🔺 *All signs in Cardiff, like this one at the station, are in both Welsh and English*

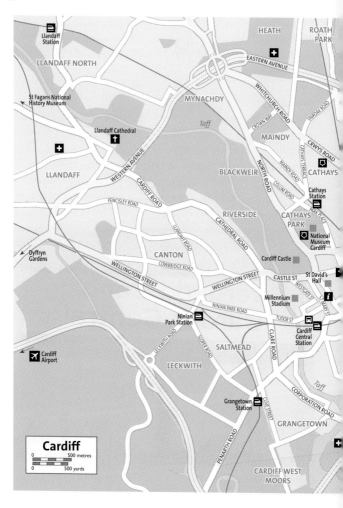

handy for the toll. Pay-and-display car parks include Castle Mews, Sophia Gardens and Cardiff Bay Barrage. For long-stay parking, head for North Road.

FINDING YOUR FEET

Laid-back, friendly and unpretentious, Cardiff doesn't present many challenges for travellers fresh off the plane. Perhaps this relaxed vibe has something to do with the youthful student population or the high concentration of green spaces providing respite from the city's buzz. Most people that arrive here soon get to grips with the sights and pace of the Welsh capital.

Another plus point for those keen to explore on foot is the pedestrianised city centre around Queen Street and the warren of Victorian arcades. Not having to dodge traffic makes walking a pleasure and takes the stress out of shopping.

As long as you have your wits about you, it's unlikely you'll experience any problems during your stay. Cardiff has a fairly low crime rate, but the general rules apply about not carrying large sums of money, or drawing unwanted attention with expensive jewellery and cameras.

ORIENTATION

Located in South Wales, Cardiff sits where the mouth of the Severn spills into the Bristol Channel. To the north lie the rolling green hills of the Valleys and Brecon Beacons (see page 132), to the west the wild Glamorgan Heritage Coast (see page 104) and the Gower Peninsula (see page 118), and to the east the English–Welsh border.

Cardiff is easy to navigate, with most of the key sights clustering in the centre, where you'll spy Cardiff Castle's towers and the almighty Millennium Stadium (see page 66). Follow Bute Street

1.6 km (1 mile) south to reach the regenerated waterfront area of Cardiff Bay (see page 76), or step north to Cathays Park, where white Portland stone buildings catch your eye.

Streets fanning out from the centre lead to Cardiff's other districts, including Roath (the student area), Heath (home to the University Hospital of Wales), Llandaff (dominated by a Norman cathedral) and St Fagans (famous for its National History Museum, see page 18). All are within an 8-km (5-mile) radius of the centre.

⏶ *Victorian landmark in terracotta red – Pierhead*

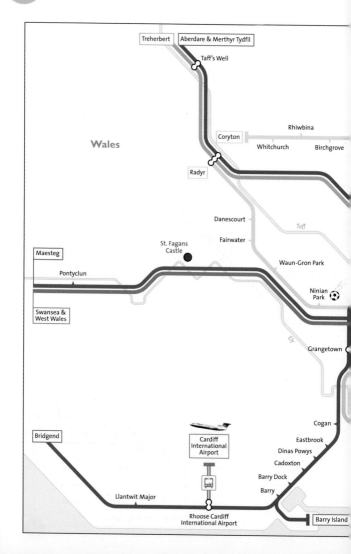

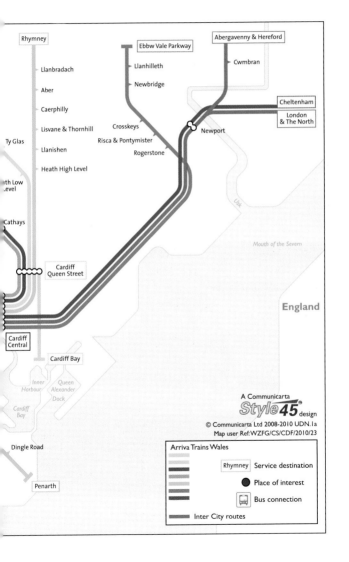

GETTING AROUND

Cardiff offers an array of transport possibilities. With pedestrianised shopping streets and most major attractions huddling in the compact city centre, the city is made for walking. If you're planning on exploring areas off the beaten tourist track, invest in the indispensable *Cardiff A–Z* street map (available at major bookshops). Of course, a bike is a great way to reach the parts cars can't and feet won't. **Cardiff Pedal Power** (ⓐ Pontcanna Fields ① (029) 2039 0713 Ⓦ www.cardiffpedalpower.org) hires out high-quality mountain bikes, as well as a range of tandemsand trikes.

Cardiff Bus operates a frequent service in and around Cardiff. You'll need the right change to buy tickets on board. For information on timetables, contact ① (029) 2066 6444 Ⓦ www.cardiffbus.com.

You can save money with a 24-hour 'Day to Go' ticket, offering unlimited travel on all bus routes.

A local rail network criss-crosses Cardiff, stopping at stations such as Queen Street, Cardiff Bay, Cathays and Llandaff. Cardiff Central links the capital to regional, national and international destinations. A laid-back way to see the sights is aboard a Cardiff Cat (see page 78). These waterbuses sail between the Cardiff Bay Barrage and Mermaid Quay. Single fares cost £2, return £4, and boats depart roughly every hour.

Around 900 licensed taxis ply Cardiff's city centre, 24/7. There are ranks at Cardiff Central Station (see page 48) and the New Theatre (Park Place) or you can hail a cab from the street. All taxis

● *Get a great view of Cardiff Bay from one of the city's waterbuses*

display signs and are equipped with a meter. Expect to pay around £5–10 for a five- to ten-minute journey.

CAR HIRE

Driving in Cardiff is not as daunting as in some capitals, but you're unlikely to need a car if you're planning to spend most of your time in the city centre. Cardiff is so compact that walking or getting around by public transport is easy and hassle-free. If you want to explore the nearby coast, valleys and mountains, having your own set of wheels is a good (but by no means the only) option. All the major car-rental agencies (including those listed below) are represented in Cardiff, either in the centre or in the short-stay car park opposite the terminal at the airport.

Avis 🅰 14–22 Tudor St ☎ 0845 544 6047 🆆 www.avis.co.uk
🕘 08.00–18.00 Mon–Fri, 08.00–13.00 Sat, closed Sun

Budget 🅰 Penarth Road ☎ (029) 2072 7499 🆆 www.budget.co.uk
🕘 08.00–18.00 Mon–Fri, 08.00–13.00 Sat, closed Sun

Europcar 🅰 At the airport ☎ (01446) 711924 🆆 www.europcar.co.uk
🕘 08.00–22.00 Mon–Fri, 08.00–16.00 Sat, 13.00–21.30 Sun

Hertz 🅰 Bessemer Road ☎ (029) 2037 5929 🆆 www.hertz.co.uk
🕘 08.00–17.30 Mon–Fri, 09.00–12.00 Sat, closed Sun

National Alamo 🅰 At the airport ☎ (01446) 719528
🆆 www.alamo.co.uk 🕘 08.00–22.30 Mon–Fri, 08.00–14.00 Sat, 13.00–21.00 Sun

Sixt 🅰 Dragon House, Coaster Place ☎ 0844 499 3399
🆆 www.sixt.co.uk 🕘 07.30–18.00 Mon–Fri, 08.00–13.30 Sat, closed Sun

---

🔾 *Cardiff's civic centre in Cathays Park*

THE CITY OF
Cardiff

Cardiff city centre

Sandwiched between Cathays and Cardiff Bay, the compact city centre is a curious blend of old and new, from the almighty Millennium Stadium (see page 66) to Cardiff Castle's stone towers and wistful turrets. Interwoven with elegant Victorian arcades and punctuated with leafy parks and modern shopping centres, the centre does trendy, traditional and everything in between. After dark, the Old Brewery Quarter is the place to party till the wee hours.

SIGHTS & ATTRACTIONS

Bute Park

This pretty park is a splash of greenery on the urban landscape. A magnet for city workers and students, this huge open space is flanked by the River Taff, Sophia Gardens, Pontcanna Fields and Cardiff Castle. Come here to chill on the riverbanks and stroll the flower gardens. ⓐ Castle St ⓣ (029) 2068 4000 ⓛ 24 hrs daily

Cardiff Castle

Sitting on 2,000 years of history, the picture-perfect castle has Roman roots but the keep is Norman. Step inside to admire the elaborate rooms decorated with stained glass, murals and marble. ⓐ Castle St ⓣ (029) 2087 8100 ⓦ www.cardiffcastle.com
ⓛ 09.00–18.00 daily (Mar–Oct); 09.00–17.00 daily (Nov–Feb)
ⓘ Admission charge

Cardiff Metropolitan Cathedral of St David

Just off Queen Street, this imposing cathedral was built in 1887 to accommodate 12,000 Catholics fleeing famine in Ireland.

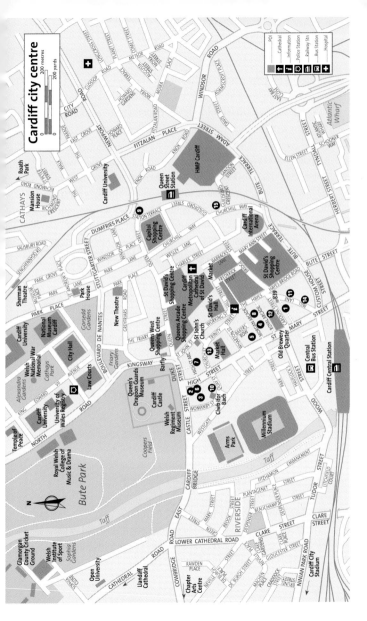

Following extensive bombing during World War II, it was rebuilt brick by brick and reopened in 1959. 📍 38 Charles St 📞 (029) 2023 1407 🌐 www.cardiffmetropolitancathedral.org.uk 🕐 24 hrs daily

Llandaff Cathedral

Set in Cardiff's leafy Llandaff district, this cathedral is one of Britain's oldest Christian sites, dating back to the 6th century. Inside, Sir Jacob Epstein's modern aluminium statue *Christ in Majesty* stands in striking contrast to the Gothic arches. It's well worth the 15-minute ride from the city centre. 📍 Cathedral Green 📞 (029) 2056 4554 🌐 www.llandaffcathedral.org.uk 🕐 24 hrs daily

Roath Park

The perfect place to escape the crowds, this central park has kept its Victorian feel. Its 12-hectare (30-acre) lake is popular for fishing and rowing. Highlights feature the subtropical greenhouse, rose and dahlia gardens, plus the lake's islands (a haven for wildlife like cormorants). The lighthouse pays tribute to Captain Scott, whose last voyage to the Antarctic began in Cardiff. 📍 Lake Road West 📞 (029) 2068 4000 🕐 07.00–dusk daily

Sophia Gardens

The city's first public park, Sophia Gardens opened in 1858. Today the grounds are home to the Glamorgan County Cricket Club and host international test matches. 📍 Cathedral Road 🕐 07.00–dusk daily

St John's Church

Seek solace from the city's buzzing shopping district at this medieval church. Sitting on the same spot for over 800 years,

⬥ *Climb up to Cardiff Castle (see page 60)*

⬥ *An oasis of calm – St John's Church*

St John's takes pride of place among Cardiff's oldest buildings and was rebuilt in the perpendicular style in the 15th century. See the light hit the slender stained-glass windows. ⓐ St John's Square
ⓣ (029) 2022 0375 ⓦ www.cardiffstjohncityparish.org.uk
ⓛ 10.00–15.00 Mon–Sat, hours of worship Sun

CULTURE

Barfly
Up-and-coming talent, budding new stars... Hot, loud and sweaty, this venue is one of the best in Cardiff for live music. ⓐ Kingsway
ⓣ 0844 847 2424 ⓦ www.barflyclub.com ⓛ Variable according to event, so phone to check

Cardiff International Arena
This vast arena is the life and soul of central Cardiff. From West End musicals to major concerts, and top comedy acts to major sporting events, the action is here. ⓐ Mary Ann St ⓣ (029) 2022 4488
ⓛ Variable according to event, so phone to check

Chapter Arts Centre
Just to the west of Cardiff in Canton, this dynamic arts centre houses a cinema, theatre, café-bar and gallery. Emphasis is on the unconventional, from physical theatre to thought-provoking plays.
ⓐ Market Road ⓣ (029) 2030 4400 ⓦ www.chapter.org ⓛ Box office 11.00–20.30 Mon–Sat, 15.00–20.30 Sun

Clwb Ifor Bach
Speak a little Welsh? Cardiff's Welsh-language club is the place to immerse yourself in the local language and culture, and enjoy

MILLENNIUM STADIUM

This iconic landmark is the face of the new city. Home to the Welsh Rugby Union, the concrete-and-steel giant is a marvel of modern technology with a fully retractable roof. Since hosting the Rugby World Cup in 1999, the Millennium Stadium has staged a string of world-class sporting events and concerts. Take a peek behind the scenes with a stadium tour. ⓐ Westgate St ❶ (029) 2082 2228 ⓦ www.millenniumstadium.com ⓛ 10.00–17.00 Mon–Sat, 10.00–16.00 Sun ❶ Admission charge

live music from rock to retro. Non-members are usually welcome, but it's worth checking on the club's noticeboard in advance. ⓐ 11 Womanby St ❶ (029) 2023 2199 ⓦ www.clwb.net ⓛ Variable according to event, so phone to check

g39

From the cutting edge to the downright controversial, this funky little gallery stages temporary exhibitions by up-and-coming Welsh artists. Expect a mix of contemporary photography, video and sculpture. ⓐ 39 Wyndham Arcade, Mill Lane ❶ (029) 2025 5541 ⓦ www.g39.org ⓛ 11.00–17.30 Wed–Sat, closed Sun–Tues

St David's Hall

High notes reverberate at the National Concert Hall of Wales, where world-class soloists, orchestras and conductors make an entrance. As well as hosting the Welsh Proms, Cardiff's key cultural venue stages dance productions and concerts, plus free exhibitions

◆ *Cardiff's Millennium Stadium*

🔺 *The Royal Arcade, home to Wally's Deli, is Cardiff's oldest arcade*

in the exhibition spaces. ⓐ The Hayes ⓣ (029) 2087 8444
ⓦ www.stdavidshallcardiff.co.uk ⓛ 09.30 until 30 mins before
start of performance Mon–Sat, closed Sun

RETAIL THERAPY

Buzz & Co Treat your feet to a pair of ultra-cool shoes. ⓐ 13 High
Street Arcade ⓣ (029) 2038 2149 ⓛ 10.00–17.30 Mon–Sat, closed Sun

Castle Welsh Crafts Pick up Welsh souvenirs at this shop opposite
the castle. ⓐ 1 Castle St ⓣ (029) 2034 3038 ⓛ 09.00–17.30 Mon–Sat,
10.00–16.00 Sun

Gallery 66 For the bigger picture, this jewel of a gallery has a
wide range of funky pop art and, as a special service, can even
print your home photos directly on to canvas. ⓐ 27–29 Royal Arcade

📞 (029) 2022 7822 🌐 www.gallerysixtysix.co.uk 🕐 10.00–17.30 Mon–Sat, closed Sun

Howells Cardiff's oldest department store where you'll find many designer brands under one roof. The food and drink section is well worth a browse. 📍 14–18 St Mary St 📞 0844 800 3713 🌐 www.houseoffraser.co.uk 🕐 09.30–18.00 Mon–Sat, 11.00–17.00 Sun

Melin Tregwynt Wrap yourself in Welsh chic with a sumptuous selection of blankets, bedspreads and throws from the world-famous designers and weavers. 📍 26 Royal Arcade 📞 (029) 2022 4997 🌐 www.melintregwynt.co.uk 🕐 10.00–17.30 Mon–Sat, closed Sun

Pussy Galore No, not a pet shop: funky club wear and gorgeous gowns. 📍 18 High Street Arcade 📞 (029) 2031 2400 🕐 10.00–17.30 Mon–Sat, 12.00–16.00 Sun

Riverside Market Local producers set up stall at this waterfront market. Fill your bags with specialities like hot Welsh cakes, honey and organic lamb, plus fruity chutneys, goat's cheese and crusty bread. 📍 Fitzhamon Embankment 📞 (029) 2019 0036 🌐 www.riversidemarket.org.uk 🕐 10.00–14.00 Sun, closed Mon–Sat

Rossiters A denizen of the Royal Arcade, Rossiters boasts an eclectic mix of furniture, china, glass and kitchen accessories alongside the very best in top brand names. 📍 33 Royal Arcade 📞 (029) 2022 4118 🌐 www.rossitersofbath.com 🕐 09.30–17.30 Mon–Sat, 12.00–16.00 Sun

Spillers Records Go to vinyl heaven at the world's oldest record shop, founded in 1894. ⓐ 31 Morgan Arcade ⓣ (029) 2022 4905 ⓦ www.spillersrecords.co.uk ⓛ 09.30–17.45 Mon–Sat, 11.30–16.00 Sun

St David's 2 The city's newest shopping centre, which houses major high-street brands, John Lewis department store and eateries including Jamie's Italian and Wagamama. ⓐ The Hayes ⓣ (029) 2036 7661 ⓦ www.stdavids2.com ⓛ 09.30–20.00 Mon–Fri, 09.30–18.00 Sat, 11.00–17.00 Sun

Wally's Delicatessen This family-run business is stacked from floor to ceiling with meats, pickles and cheeses alongside oodles of Chinese, Thai and Mexican products. ⓐ 38–46 Royal Arcade ⓣ (029) 2022 9265 ⓦ www.wallysdeli.co.uk ⓛ 08.00–17.30 Mon–Sat, 11.00–16.00 Sun

TAKING A BREAK

Ask Cardiff £ ❶ Bright and buzzing, this restaurant is the perfect pizza pit stop. ⓐ 24–32 Wyndham Arcade, Mill Lane ⓣ (029) 2034 4665 ⓛ 12.00–23.00 Sun–Thur, 12.00–23.30 Fri & Sat

Café Minuet £ ❷ Authentic Italian fare and the finest cappuccino in town. ⓐ 42 Castle Arcade ⓣ (029) 2034 1794 ⓛ 11.00–16.30 Mon–Sat, closed Sun

Cegin Y Ddraig £ ❸ The 'Dragon's Kitchen' is the place to go for good-value home-made Welsh staples such as *cawl* (lamb stew), Welsh rarebit and *bara brith* (spiced fruit loaf). They do takeaways, too. ❷ 47–49 Castle Arcade ❶ (029) 2023 3723 ❸ 08.00–17.30 Mon–Fri, 09.00–17.30 Sat, closed Sun

Harleys £ ❹ If the bright yellow décor doesn't cheer you up, then the sandwiches, toasties, snacks and traditional Welsh cakes most certainly will! ❷ 8 Royal Arcade ❶ (029) 2037 3816 ❸ 07.00–14.30 Mon–Sat, closed Sun

The Louis Restaurant £ ❺ Fill up on good-value home-made food at this laid-back restaurant. ❷ 32 St Mary St ❶ (029) 2022 5722 ❸ 08.30–19.30 Mon–Sat, 10.00–16.30 Sun

Madame Fromage £ ❻ A café (and shop) with a distinct French twist. Sample the range of superior wines, bread, local (and exotic) cheeses, olives and meats, jams and chutneys. ❷ 21–25 Castle Arcade ❶ (029) 2064 4888 ❾ www.madamefromage.co.uk ❸ 10.00–17.30 Mon–Fri, 09.30–17.30 Sat, 12.00–17.00 Sun

New York Deli £ ❼ The sandwiches at this deli are enormous and the bagels take some beating, too. ❷ 19 High Street Arcade ❶ (029) 2038 8388 ❸ 09.00–17.00 Mon–Sat, closed Sun

Plan Café £ ❽ It's never hard to find a window seat in this goldfish-bowl-style café. It serves fresh, seasonal organic soups and light meals. The pancakes are the best in town. ❷ 28–29 Morgan Arcade ❶ (029) 2039 8764 ❸ 09.00–17.00 Mon–Sat, 11.00–16.00 Sun

Zushi £ ❾ Eat sushi and surf the web at this funky Japanese noodle bar. ❷ 140 Queen St ❶ (029) 2066 9911 ❾ www.zushicardiff.com ❸ 12.00–22.00 Mon–Sat, 12.00–17.00 Sun

AFTER DARK

RESTAURANTS

Casanova £ ❿ Don't expect pizza or spag bol from the finest Italian restaurant in the city. Do expect plenty of traditional Neapolitan dishes made with local ingredients. ⓐ 13 Quay St ❶ (029) 2034 4044 Ⓦ www.casanovacardiff.com ❷ 12.00–14.30, 17.30–22.00 Mon–Sat, closed Sun

Las Iguanas £ ⓫ Brazilian lime chicken and potent *caipirinha* cocktails make this prime party territory. Go Latino and dine before dancing downstairs. ⓐ 8 Mill Lane ❶ (029) 2022 6373 Ⓦ www.iguanas.co.uk ❷ 12.00–23.00 Sun–Thur, 12.00–23.30 Fri & Sat

Spice Quarter £ ⓬ Tangy massalas and fiery vindaloos whet appetites at this sleek and central Indian restaurant. Vegetarian menus are available. ⓐ Old Brewery Quarter ❶ (029) 2022 0075 Ⓦ www.spicequarter.co.uk ❷ 12.00–14.30, 17.00–22.30 daily

Ten Feet Tall £ ⓭ Fashionable venue set over three floors where you can enjoy tapas and shared platters inspired by the Med and North Africa. There's a DJ and/or live music every night until 04.00. ⓐ 11a–12 Church St ❶ (029) 2022 8883 ❷ Food served 11.00–21.00 Sun–Wed, 11.00–22.00 Thur–Sat

La Brasserie ££ ⓮ Fashionable, buzzy restaurant with a Spanish vibe serving up grilled meat and fish. Outdoor terrace. ⓐ Mill Lane ❶ (029) 2023 4134 Ⓦ www.le-monde.co.uk ❷ 12.00–14.30, 19.00–24.00 Tues–Thur, 12.00–02.00 Fri & Sat, closed Sun & Mon

The Thai House Restaurant ££ **⑮** Spicy curries and steaming noodles lure punters to this award-winning restaurant. Ingredients are fresh, service efficient and the wine list impressive. **ⓐ** 3–5 Guildford Crescent **ⓣ** (029) 2038 7404 **ⓦ** www.thaihouse.biz **ⓛ** 12.00–14.30, 18.00–22.30 Mon–Sat, closed Sun

BARS & CLUBS

Bogiez Fans of heavy rock and metal should head to this club night, which takes place in the shadow of the Millennium Stadium on the first and third Saturday of every month. **ⓐ** Millennium Music Hall, Wood St **ⓦ** www.bogiez.com **ⓛ** 22.00–04.00 daily

Buffalo Very cool venue showcasing up-and-coming bands. DJs spin hip hop and dance on Fridays and Saturdays. **ⓐ** 11 Windsor Place **ⓦ** www.buffalobar.com **ⓛ** 20.00–03.00 Mon–Thur, 22.00–04.00 Fri–Sun

Café Floyd Blink and you might miss this tiny bar whose scene is set by dark wooden floors, leather sofas and soul music. The cocktails are excellent and the vibe chilled. **ⓐ** 23 High St **ⓣ** (029) 2022 2181 **ⓦ** www.cafefloyd.co.uk **ⓛ** 19.30–03.00 Thur–Sat, closed Sun–Wed

Café Jazz Plenty of sax appeal at this laid-back venue, staging top-quality jazz and blues gigs most nights. **ⓐ** 21 St Mary St **ⓣ** (029) 2038 7026 **ⓦ** www.cafejazzcardiff.com **ⓛ** 11.30–23.30 daily

Copa This relaxed bar serves continental beers, including cherry-flavoured Kriek. **ⓐ** 4 Wharton St **ⓣ** (029) 2022 2114 **ⓛ** 11.30–23.00 Mon–Wed, 11.30–24.00 Thur, 11.30–01.00 Fri & Sat, 12.00–22.00 Sun

The Goat Major Sit back in a leather armchair and enjoy a pint of Brains in one of Cardiff's legendary pubs. Its name refers to the mascot of the 41st Regiment of Wales – a live goat carried on the front line in the Crimean War! ⓐ High Street
ⓣ (029) 2033 7161 ⓛ 12.00–24.00 Mon–Sat, 12.00–22.00 Sun

Lava Lounge Try a zesty Lava Cooler at this real-life Club Tropicana.
ⓐ Old Brewery Quarter, St Mary St ⓣ (029) 2038 2313

🔺 *Sample the local brew, Brains beer, at The Yard*

Ⓦ www.lavalounge.co.uk Ⓛ 14.00–01.00 Fri, 12.00–03.00 Sat, 20.00–04.00 Sun, closed Mon–Thur

Prince of Wales Enjoy a swift pint then attempt the spiral staircases at this Wetherspoon's pub that's set in an old theatre. Ⓐ 82 St Mary St Ⓣ (029) 2064 4449 Ⓛ 07.00–24.00 Sun–Thur, 07.00–01.00 Fri & Sat

Reflex Kitsch but fun, this is a refreshing change from the city's trendy bars. Come here if you want to let your hair down and boogie to eighties' hits. Ⓐ 89 St Mary St Ⓣ (029) 2066 8647 Ⓦ www.reflexbars.co.uk Ⓛ 21.00–02.00 Mon–Wed, 20.00–02.00 Thur, 20.00–03.00 Fri & Sat, 20.00–01.00 Sun

Soda This trendy bar does urban chic well, with cave-like cubby holes, exposed brick and a black-and-white colour scheme. Ⓐ 7–10 Mill Lane Ⓣ (029) 2023 8181 Ⓦ www.thesodabar.com Ⓛ 22.00–02.00 Thur, 22.00–03.00 Fri, 22.00–04.00 Sat, closed Sun–Wed

The Toucan Club Tipped as the friendliest bar and music venue in town. There's a lively club atmosphere, thanks to an eclectic mix of hip hop and Latin dance. It also serves pizza. Ⓐ 23 Womanby St Ⓣ 07850 461684 Ⓦ www.toucancardiff.co.uk Ⓛ 18.00–04.00 Tues–Sun, closed Mon

The Yard The offspring of Brains Brewery, this huge bar has industrial décor and serves Brains bitters and ales, plus value-for-money food. Ⓐ 42–43 St Mary St Ⓣ (029) 2022 7577 Ⓦ www.yardbarkitchen.co.uk Ⓛ 10.00–23.00 Mon–Thur, 10.00–02.00 Fri–Sun

Cardiff Bay

Seeing the Water Tower glint, the Wales Millennium Centre
(see page 83) rise proud and the trendy glass-walled bars lining
Mermaid Quay, it's hard to believe that Cardiff Bay was ever the
coal-exporting hub it once was. But this Tiger is burning bright
again, thanks to a multi-million-pound makeover. Welcome to
modern Cardiff, a place of cutting-edge architecture, fizzing cocktail
bars and ever-so-posh boutiques. Yet scratch beneath the surface
and you'll find that the past is still very much alive.

The area is well served by three Cardiff Bus (see page 56) services,
numbers 6 (the Baycar bendy-bus), 8 and 35. You could also catch the
Aquabus (❶ (029) 2047 2004 ❿ www.aquabus.co.uk) from the River
Taff at Cardiff Castle to Mermaid Quay.

SIGHTS & ATTRACTIONS

Cardiff Bay Barrage

A marvel of modern engineering, the barrage's 40-m (131-ft)
locks and bascule bridges have created a 200-hectare (494-acre)
freshwater lake fed by the rivers Taff and Ely. Explore the embankment
and get the best views of the waterfront from Barrage Point,
shaped like a ship's bow. ❸ Cardiff Bay ❶ (029) 2070 0234
❿ www.cardiffharbour.com ● 07.00–22.00 daily (summer);
08.00–16.00 daily (winter)

Cardiff Bay Visitor Centre

Dubbed 'The Tube', this futuristic visitor centre is an attraction in
its own right. The brainchild of architect William Alsop, the award-
winning design built of steel and plywood is in the shape of a giant

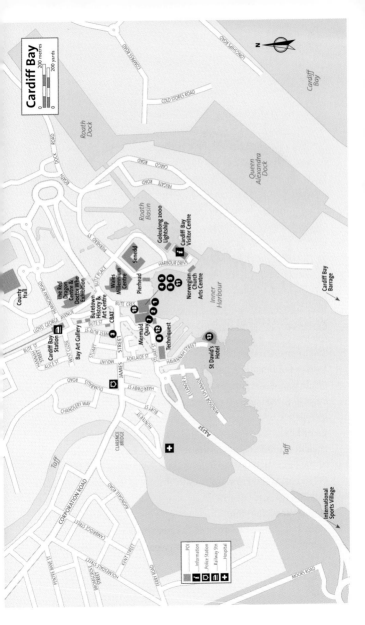

⬥ *Start your visit at 'The Tube', the Cardiff Bay Visitor Centre*

telescope. Step inside to take in a free exhibition and admire views of the bay. Tourist information and maps are available. ⓐ Harbour Drive ⓣ (029) 2046 3833 ⓛ 10.00–18.00 daily

Cardiff Cats
Soak up Cardiff's sights from the water on a 30-minute mini-cruise of the bay. Hop on at Mermaid Quay or Penarth. ⓐ Cardiff Bay ⓣ (07940) 142409 ⓦ www.cardiffcats.com ⓛ 10.00–16.30 daily

Doctor Who Exhibition
Since 2005 the cult sci-fi series has been mainly filmed in and around Cardiff. This exhibition features costumes, monsters and props from

the last few series and is a must-visit for fans. ⓐ The Red Dragon
Centre ① (029) 2048 9257 Ⓦ www.doctorwhoexhibition.com
🕒 10.00–18.30 daily ① Admission charge

Goleulong 2000 Lightship

This huge red-and-white vessel moored in Cardiff Bay was last
stationed off Rhossili on the Gower Peninsula. Effectively a floating
church, the vessel now has a peaceful chapel on board. It's free
to explore the engine room, cabins and deck. ⓐ Harbour Drive
① (029) 2048 7609 Ⓦ www.lightship2000.co.uk 🕒 10.00–17.00
Mon–Sat, 14.00–17.00 Sun

Norwegian Church Arts Centre

Once a Norwegian seafarers' church in Butetown, this pretty white
chapel was moved brick by brick to Cardiff Bay in 1992. Famous
children's author Roald Dahl was baptised here in 1916. The intimate
venue now houses an art gallery and concert hall staging early
music, folk and jazz performances. Rest your feet in the café by the
waterfront. ⓐ Harbour Drive ① (029) 2087 7959
Ⓦ www.norwegianchurchcardiff.com 🕒 10.00–17.00 daily

Pierhead

The terracotta towers and silver turrets of the Pierhead date back to
1897. The Victorian interior, clock tower and interactive exhibition are
highlights of a visit. ⓐ Maritime Road ① 0845 010 5500
Ⓦ http://pierhead.org 🕒 10.30–16.30 Mon–Sat, closed Sun

Senedd (National Assembly for Wales)

The National Assembly for Wales dominates the waterfront with
its smooth contours and wave-shaped roof. The energy-efficient

structure cost a cool £67 million to build and uses the earth for heat and a wind cowl for ventilation. Modern art features include 32 glass panels forming *The Assembly Field* and the fibre-optic *Heart of Wales* set in the chamber's oak floor. Visit the roof to see the debating chamber through the funnel's round windows. ⓐ Harbour Drive ⓣ 0845 010 5500 ⓦ www.wales.gov.uk ⓛ 09.30–16.30 Mon & Fri, 08.00–end of business Tues–Thur (term time); 09.30–16.30 Mon–Fri (recess), 10.30–16.30 Sat & Sun (all year)

Techniquest

Scintillating science is the focus of this hands-on discovery museum. Behind glass walls, kids (and big kids) can test out 160 interactive exhibits from firing a rocket to launching a hot-air balloon, experimenting in the laboratory, or simply studying the stars in the planetarium. ⓐ Stuart St ⓣ (029) 2047 5475 ⓦ www.techniquest.org ⓛ 09.30–16.30 Mon–Fri, 10.00–17.00 Sat & Sun ⓘ Admission charge

CULTURE

Bay Art Gallery

Pause at this airy gallery to enjoy exhibitions featuring paintings and sculpture by contemporary Welsh and international artists. ⓐ 54b/c Bute St ⓣ (029) 2065 0016 ⓦ www.bayart.org.uk ⓛ 12.00–17.00 Tues–Sat, closed Sun & Mon

Butetown History & Art Centre

Focusing on the voice of the people, this pioneering centre traces local history through photography, art exhibitions, video screenings, life stories and tours. A visit here is a great way to discover more

⬥ *The Goleulong 2000 Lightship in Cardiff Bay*

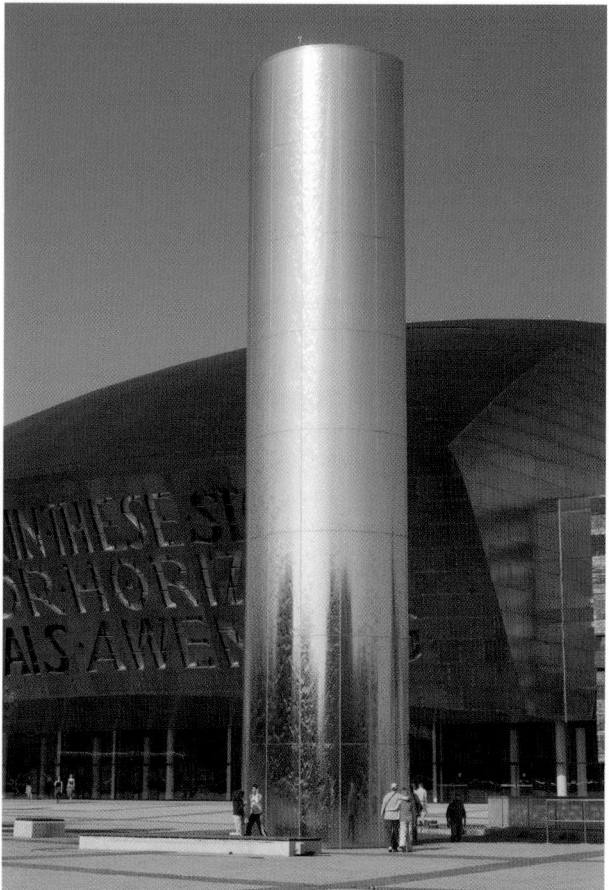

The Wales Millennium Centre with its stunning fountain

about Cardiff Docklands' fascinating past. ⓐ 5 Dock Chambers, Bute St ⓣ (029) 2025 6757 ⓦ www.bhac.org ⓛ 10.00–17.00 Tues–Fri, 11.00–16.30 Sat & Sun, closed Mon

CBAT

Explore Welsh, British and international art on canvas at this avant-garde gallery. The backbone behind a number of public regeneration schemes, the venue's concept is for art to bring the urban landscape to life. Exhibitions are free. ⓐ 123 Bute St ⓣ 0845 241 3684 ⓦ www.cbat.co.uk ⓛ 10.00–17.00 Tues–Fri, closed Sat–Mon

Wales Millennium Centre

The darling of the bay's performing-arts scene, this iconic slate-and-steel building stages world-class opera, ballet, dance and musicals, including performances by the resident Welsh National Opera. The venue hosts free lunchtime and early evening concerts most days. ⓐ Bute Place ⓣ Box office (029) 2063 6464 ⓦ www.wmc.org.uk ⓛ 10.00–18.00 Mon–Fri, 11.00–17.00 Sat & Sun

RETAIL THERAPY

Castle Galleries Affordable originals, prints and sculptures presented in a modern feel. A good mix of contemporary and traditional work, including pieces from local artists. ⓐ Unit 21, Mermaid Quay ⓣ (029) 2049 5240 ⓦ www.castlegalleries.com ⓛ 10.00–18.00 Mon–Sat, 11.00–17.00 Sun

Craft in the Bay (Makers Guild) This attractive gallery set in a Grade-II-listed warehouse is the place to find everything from handwoven wicker to a beautifully embroidered bodice, as well as

CARDIFF INTERNATIONAL SPORTS VILLAGE

If any one scheme illustrates Cardiff's current level of confidence and ambition, it's the city's waterfront International Sports Village. The £700-million project will, by the time it is completed, make Cardiff a world-class sports centre. Some buildings are already open, including a fabulous 50-m (55-yd) swimming pool and adjacent leisure pool, a temporary ice rink and a white-water rafting and kayaking centre. There will eventually be a snow dome for skiers and boarders. Take bus number 9 from the city centre. ❸ Olympian Drive

fine prints, textiles, jewellery and ceramics. It also offers a wide range of creative courses. ❸ The Flourish, Lloyd George Av ❶ (029) 2048 4611 Ⓦ www.makersguildinwales.org.uk Ⓛ 10.30–17.30 daily

Fabulous Welshcakes Not only does this shop stock delicious, award-winning Welshcakes but you'll also find a range of regional arts and crafts – lovespoons, Welsh slate, handmade chocolates and books by Welsh authors. ❸ Unit 14, Mermaid Quay ❶ (029) 2045 6593 Ⓦ www.fabulouswelshcakes.co.uk Ⓛ 10.30–17.30 Mon–Sat, 11.00–17.00 Sun

Portmeirion As well as a range of designer gifts, books and official Wales Millennium Centre souvenirs, this smartly laid-out shop also sells the world-famous Portmeirion pottery and glassware. ❸ Wales Millennium Centre, Bute Place ❶ (029) 2047 0460 Ⓦ www.portmeirion-village.com Ⓛ 10.00–18.00 daily

TAKING A BREAK

Cadwalader's £ ❶ Ice cream at its best, and pioneering: try such *gelato* innovations as chocolate porridge. ⓐ Unit 30, Mermaid Quay ⓣ (029) 2049 7598 ⓦ www.cadwaladersicecream.co.uk ⓛ 10.00–22.00 daily (summer); 10.00–17.00 daily (winter)

Coffee Mania £ ❷ Whether you're after a frothy coffee or a sushi and salad, this spherical café is a top choice. ⓐ Unit 29, Mermaid Quay ⓣ (029) 2046 4546 ⓛ 07.30–22.00 daily

Gorge with George £ ❸ The no-nonsense menu at this unassuming little place includes hearty cooked breakfasts that really hit the spot. ⓐ 15 West Bute St ⓣ (029) 2045 6887 ⓛ 07.30–14.00 Mon–Fri, 08.00–11.30 Sat, closed Sun

Herb & Ellie's £ ❹ Relax in stylish vintage surroundings with a gourmet coffee and a slice of yummy cake. They do sandwiches and salads, too. ⓐ Unit 11, Mermaid Quay ⓣ (029) 2045 5955 ⓛ 08.00–17.30 Mon–Fri, 08.00–18.00 Sat & Sun

Garcon! £–££ ❺ With fantastic views across the bay, this French-style brasserie's authentic menu includes bistro favourites, platters to share, steak tartare and the signature dish, cassoulet. ⓐ Upper Unit 9, Mermaid Quay ⓣ (029) 2049 0990 ⓦ www.garcon-resto.co.uk ⓛ 12.00–22.00 Mon–Thur, 12.00–23.00 Fri & Sat, 12.00–17.00 Sun

Bellini's ££ ❻ Minimalist chic sums up this smart Italian restaurant overlooking Mermaid Quay, offering special lunch menus. Try the

sea bass or freshly baked pizza. ❸ Upper Unit 10, Mermaid Quay
❶ (029) 2048 7070 Ⓦ www.bellinisitaliano.com ❶ 12.00–15.30,
18.00–22.30 daily

AFTER DARK

RESTAURANTS

Mimosa Kitchen & Bar £ ❼ This tastefully designed corner
restaurant oozes style, with its long, wood-panelled bar and
chocolate-coloured seating. The menu has a strong Welsh
accent, including *cawl*, and uses locally sourced organic ingredients.
❸ Mermaid Quay ❶ (029) 2049 1900 Ⓦ www.mimosakitchen.co.uk
❶ 10.00–22.00 Mon–Sat, 10.00–21.30 Sun

Spice Merchant Cardiff Bay £ ❽ This modern restaurant decked
out in bold reds and blues offers authentic Indian fare with a twist.
The menu promises spicy food and natural ingredients. It delivers.
❸ The Big Windsor, Stuart St ❶ (029) 2049 8984
Ⓦ www.spicemerchantcardiff.co.uk ❶ 11.30–23.30 daily

Signor Valentino's £–££ ❾ Oak flooring, open-plan kitchen,
contemporary art and floor-to-ceiling glass make this modern
restaurant a favourite among Cardiff's hipsters. Prices are
affordable and the Italian food delicious. ❸ Unit 15, Mermaid Quay
❶ (029) 2048 2007 Ⓦ www.signorvalentino.com ❶ 12.00–22.30
Mon–Thur, 12.00–23.00 Fri–Sun

Moksh ££ ❿ Indian cuisine with a contemporary feel from this
highly rated eatery. With sumptuous red, orange and brown décor,
Moksh serves authentic dishes with a modern twist. Advanced

booking recommended. ⓐ Ocean Buildings, Bute Crescent ❶ (029) 2049 8120 Ⓦ www.mokshrestaurant.co.uk 🕒 12.00–14.30, 18.00– 23.00 Mon–Thur, 12.00–14.30, 18.00–24.00 Fri & Sat, 18.00–24.00 Sun

Pearl of the Orient ££ ⓫ Light and airy Chinese restaurant where you can enjoy a wide range of dishes accompanied by live piano music most evenings. ⓐ First Floor, Mermaid Quay ❶ (029) 2049 8080 Ⓦ www.thepearloftheorient.com 🕒 12.00–15.00, 17.00–23.00 Mon–Fri, 12.00–23.00 Sat, 12.00–22.30 Sun

Woods Brasserie ££ ⓬ Top-end eatery set in stylish and minimalist surroundings, oft frequented by the bay's business and political community. A diverse menu encompasses the best of British, Mediterranean and Asian cuisine. ⓐ Pilotage Building, Stuart St ❶ (029) 2049 2400 Ⓦ www.woods-brasserie.com 🕒 12.00–14.00, 17.30–22.00 Mon–Sat, 12.00–15.00, 19.00–22.00 (June–Sept only) Sun

Tempus £££ ⓭ The 5-star cuisine tempts foodies to St David's Hotel & Spa. If your bank balance won't stretch to dinner, enjoy the same views over afternoon tea. ⓐ Havannah St ❶ (029) 2045 4045 Ⓦ www.thestdavidshotel.com 🕒 12.30–21.30 daily

BARS & CLUBS

Ba Orient Step into the East at this atmospheric dim sum and cocktail bar. The low lighting and floor-to-ceiling Chinese lanterns set the mood for a relaxing meal or romantic drinks. ⓐ Mermaid Quay ❶ (029) 2046 3939 Ⓦ www.baorient.com 🕒 12.00–23.00 Mon, 12.00–24.00 Tues–Thur, 12.00–01.00 Fri, 13.00–02.00 Sat, 13.00–23.00 Sun

Bute Dock No airs and graces, this is just a good, old-fashioned watering hole with darts, occasional live music and a beer garden. ⓐ West Bute St ⓣ (029) 2065 1426 ⓛ 12.00–23.00 Mon–Sat, 12.00–23.30 Sun

Eli Jenkins This modern, upmarket pub draws an arty crowd and serves a decent selection of real ales. ⓐ 7–8 Bute Crescent ⓣ (029) 2044 0921 ⓛ 11.00–23.30 Mon–Sat, 11.00–22.30 Sun

Grosvenor Casino If you're feeling lucky, try your hand at poker, blackjack and roulette or hit the slot machines. Make a night of it and book a table in the restaurant. ⓐ The Red Dragon Centre ⓣ (029) 2046 8350 ⓦ www.thereddragoncentre.co.uk ⓛ 24 hrs daily

Mischiefs Café Bar A stylish lunch venue by day and a lively place to enjoy a drink in the evening. There's live music on Friday and Saturday. ⓐ 36 James St ⓣ (029) 2045 6111 ⓦ www.mischiefs.co.uk ⓛ 10.00–24.00 daily

Salt Right on the waterfront, this bar-cum-restaurant is always packed. Cocktails are creatively slung together, and the atmosphere is buzzing. ⓐ Mermaid Quay ⓣ (029) 2049 4375 ⓦ www.saltcardiff.com ⓛ 11.00–23.00 Sun–Thur, 11.00–02.00 Fri & Sat

Terra Nova Shaped like a ship's bow, this glam addition to Cardiff Bay has slender glass windows and stylish balconies. Few places can beat the views and sparkling Chardonnay on a summer's evening. ⓐ Mermaid Quay ⓣ (029) 2045 0947 ⓦ www.terranovacardiff.com ⓛ 10.00–23.00 Sun–Thur, 10.00–02.00 Fri & Sat

🔺 *Start your big night out at cool Salt – or Terra Nova across the street*

The Waterguard As the sign outside states: 'It's a pub. And it's open.'
Thirsty punters looking for quality beers, a laid-back atmosphere
and somewhere quiet enough to have a good chat are in the right
place. ⓐ Harbour Drive ⓣ (029) 2049 9034 ⓒ 12.00–23.00 Mon–Sat,
12.00–22.30 Sun

The Wharf An impressive red-brick building houses this
sprawling bar and restaurant. There's live music on Friday and
Saturday. ⓐ 121 Schooner Way ⓣ (029) 2040 5092
ⓦ www.thewharfcardiff.com ⓒ 12.00–23.30 Sun–Thur, 11.00–01.00
Fri & Sat

Cathays

Cathays is pinned at the capital's civic heart. While most visitors make a beeline for the vast National Museum Cardiff (see page 96), it's worth lingering to see what else this corner of Cardiff has to offer, especially in Cathays Park, the old administrative centre of the city, with its beautiful architecture and elegant squares. The wealth that the coal industry brought during the 19th century is reflected here in the manicured gardens and fine Edwardian buildings, avant-garde theatres and captivating art galleries.

The area is well served by Cardiff Bus (see page 56) service number 29.

SIGHTS & ATTRACTIONS

Alexandra Gardens

This pocket of greenery is a pleasant spot in which to relax beside the flowers and cedar trees, and watch the world go by. The garden is at its best in spring, when it's awash with tulips and pink cherry blossom. ⓐ Cathays Park ⓛ 24 hrs daily

Cardiff University

You can't fail to miss the impressive white-stone building of the main campus in the civic centre. If you want to enter the campus, get permission from the porters first. ⓐ Park Place ⓣ (029) 2087 4000 ⓦ www.cardiff.ac.uk

Cathays Cemetery

One of Britain's largest Victorian cemeteries, this atmospheric site spans over 40 hectares (100 acres). The 3-km (2-mile) Heritage Trail

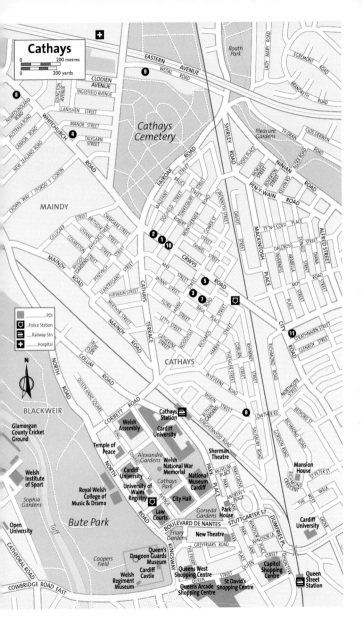

traces the cemetery's history, taking a glimpse at Cardiff's famous past residents and memorials. **ⓐ** Fairoak Road **ⓛ** 24 hrs daily

City Hall

A Welsh dragon perches on the domed roof of this Renaissance-style building, carved from white Portland stone. A sweeping staircase leads to the Marble Hall, housing 11 marble statues of Welsh heroes, including St David. The extensive art collection, oak-panelled Council Chamber and ornate Assembly Rooms are also worth a visit. **ⓐ** Cathays Park **ⓣ** (029) 2087 1727 **ⓦ** www.cardiffcityhall.com **ⓛ** 09.00–17.00 Mon–Fri, closed Sat & Sun (subject to change)

Friary Gardens

These small but perfectly formed gardens are framed with neat hedges and clipped bushes, planted in honour of the third Marquess of Bute. A break here provides respite from the city's buzz. **ⓐ** Cathays Park **ⓛ** 24 hrs daily

Gorsedd Gardens

Stroll shady paths in these gardens, one of Cardiff's best-kept secrets. Spy the bronze statues of Lord Ninian Stuart and John Cory rising from the bushes, and the famous Gorsedd Circle – a ceremonial set of stones that has been a feature of the park since 1899. **ⓐ** Cathays Park

Law Courts

Standing in leafy Cathays Park and flanking the City Hall, the city's grand Law Courts date back to 1904. Glimpse the obelisk-style lamps bearing Cardiff's coat of arms and the statue of Judge Gwilym Williams. **ⓐ** Cathays Park

AMGUEDDFA GENEDLAETHOL CYMRU

△ The National Museum Cardiff has a superb Impressionist collection (see page 96)

⬧ *Stop for a moment at the Welsh National War Memorial*

Park House

This Gothic-style gem, completed in 1875, was the brainchild of acclaimed architect William Burges. Today the grey sandstone building is one of Cardiff's most iconic 19th-century town houses. It's now a private members' club. **a** 20 Park Place **t** (029) 2022 4343 **w** www.parkhouseclub.com

Temple of Peace

A gift from Lord David Davies of Llandinam to the Welsh people, this classical T-shaped building pays homage to those who lost their lives in World War I. The red-roofed structure shelters the marble Temple Hall, wood-panelled Council Chamber and the Crypt housing the first Welsh *Book of Remembrance*, which, at 1,100 pages long, contains the names of 35,000 Welsh men and women. Dr Who enthusiasts may like to know it has been used as a location in several episodes. **a** Cathays Park

University of Wales Registry

Spot Cathays Park's first building, characterised by its Ionic columns, round windows and ever-photogenic sleeping dragons adorning the front posts. **a** King Edward VII Av

Welsh National War Memorial

At Alexandra Gardens' centre, you'll find this sunken court with Corinthian columns. The memorial was designed by Sir Ninian Cooper and unveiled in June 1928. The three bronze figures (a soldier, a sailor and an airman) commemorate the men who lost their lives in World War I, and are topped by a winged nude representing victory. **a** Alexandra Gardens

CULTURE

New Theatre

Entertainment is synonymous with this Edwardian venue, whether your idea of a good night out is a glitzy West End show, modern ballet or poignant drama. This is also the place to head for Cardiff's star-studded Christmas pantomime. ⓐ Park Place ⓣ (029) 2087 8889 ⓦ www.newtheatrecardiff.co.uk ⓛ Variable according to event, so phone to check

Sherman Theatre

Youth theatre is the essence of this energetic performing-arts venue. The programme is a fusion of experimental productions, drama adaptations and family musicals. One of the major cultural venues in South Wales, the theatre has a resident company that cultivates new talent. ⓐ Senghennydd Road ⓣ (029) 2064 6900 ⓦ www.shermancymru.co.uk ⓛ Variable according to event, so phone to check

NATIONAL MUSEUM CARDIFF

Moving from art gems to archaeology and from natural history to geology, this superb museum is a cultural highlight of any visit to Cardiff, showcasing one of Europe's best Impressionist collections. Highlights stretch from Picasso prints to contemporary Welsh stoneware. Children love the Evolution of Wales, tracing the country's history back millions of years to the age of dinosaurs. ⓐ Cathays Park ⓣ (029) 2039 7951 ⓦ www.museumwales.ac.uk ⓛ 10.00–17.00 Tues–Sun, closed Mon

⬤ *Take in a show at the New Theatre*

TAKING A BREAK

Aroma Café £ ❶ Cardiff's first halal café, which also does a nice line in yummy cakes and creamy milkshakes. **ⓐ** 126 Crwys Road **ⓣ** (029) 2022 2055 **ⓛ** 09.00–19.00 Mon–Sat, 09.45–18.00 Sun

Café Calcio £ ❷ A down-to-earth café with friendly atmosphere and generous portions: the bangers and mash, fry-ups and quick curries score highly. **ⓐ** 145 Crwys Road **ⓣ** (029) 2039 7575 **ⓛ** 09.00–16.30 daily

Café Junior £ ❸ Families flock to this light-filled café, where adults can sip cappuccinos on comfy sofas while the little ones play. The healthy menu is mostly organic. **ⓐ** Fanny St **ⓣ** (029) 2034 5653 **ⓦ** www.cafejunior.com **ⓛ** 09.30–18.00 daily

Café Mao £ ❹ Slip into the low, comfy sofas for some exquisite Mediterranean-style food and a chilled-out vibe. Portions are on the large side, so slipping out of the sofas could be a challenge. **ⓐ** 90–92 Whitchurch Road **ⓣ** (029) 2039 8433 **ⓛ** 08.30–16.00 Mon–Sat, 11.00–15.00 Sun

Café Mina £ ❺ For a Lebanese lunch, this relaxed restaurant beckons. Munch on meze and spicy meatballs. **ⓐ** 43 Crwys Road **ⓣ** (029) 2023 5212 **ⓦ** www.cafemina.co.uk **ⓛ** 17.00–23.00 daily

Cocorico Patisserie £ ❻ To the west of Cathays Cemetery, this French café is the place to go for mouthwatering cakes and great sandwiches. **ⓐ** 55a Whitchurch Road **ⓣ** (029) 2132 8177 **ⓛ** 09.00–17.30 Mon–Sat, closed Sun

AFTER DARK

RESTAURANTS

Aegean Taverna £ ❼ This lively restaurant serves tasty Greek food with copious amounts of retsina. Sample specialities like stuffed calamari and meze, rounded off with sticky baklava. ❸ 117 Woodville Road ❶ (029) 2034 5114 Ⓦ www.aegeantaverna.co.uk ❻ 18.45–23.00 Mon–Sat, closed Sun

Fortune House £ ❽ Expect generous portions, great Chinese food and friendly staff. The all-you-can-eat emperor's choice menu comes recommended. ❸ 43–45 Salisbury Road ❶ (029) 2064 1311 Ⓦ www.fortunehouse.co.uk ❻ 12.00–14.00, 17.30–23.30 Mon–Sat, closed Sun

Grape and Olive £ ❾ On the north side of Cathays Cemetery, this bright, contemporary restaurant serves up Mediterranean cuisine to a lively clientele. ❸ 39 Wedal Road ❶ (029) 2061 7054 Ⓦ www.grapeandolive.co.uk ❻ 10.00–23.00 daily

Phi-b's £ ❿ Enjoy authentic Chinese with a modern twist at this sleek venue complete with Chinatown-style frontage, a favourite among those craving a little spice. ❸ 98 Crwys Road ❶ (029) 2039 8352 Ⓦ www.phi-bs.co.uk ❻ 17.00–23.00 Mon–Thur, 12.00–14.00, 17.00–24.00 Fri–Sun

Tenkaichi £ ⓫ Japanese fare served on canteen-style tables; ideal for bigger groups or even as a way of meeting new friends. The bento boxes have a good selection, with plenty of sushi rolls to choose from and oodles of noodle dishes.

ⓐ 236 City Road **ⓣ** (029) 2048 1888 **ⓦ** www.tenkaichi.co.uk
ⓛ 12.00–14.00, 17.30–23.00 Mon–Thur, 12.00–24.00 Fri & Sat,
12.00–22.30 Sun

BARS & CLUBS

Bar En Route Small and intimate bar that offers a huge selection of
wines and more than 60 imported bottled beers. For traditionalists,
there's a good selection of real ales from established and micro
breweries. **ⓐ** 138a Cathays Terrace **ⓣ** (07960) 005300
ⓛ 19.00–23.00 Mon–Sat, closed Sun

Cardiff Arts Institute As its name suggests, this is the place to go for
obscure bands, experimental paintings, storytelling, fancy dress
parties and African beats – if you think you're hip enough.
ⓐ 29 Park Place **ⓣ** (029) 2023 1252 **ⓦ** http://cardiffartsinstitute.org
ⓛ 12.00–24.00 daily

The Crockerton By day, a dinky bar where the chink of ice cubes
almost drowns out the muzak. By night, a happening club that
pumps out classy dance fodder. **ⓐ** Greyfriars Road **ⓣ** (029) 2037 5600
ⓛ 07.00–02.00 Sun–Wed, 07.00–02.30 Thur–Sat

Exit Bar A fabulously out-there club that's gay in every sense of the
word, but there's nothing to frighten the horses here, and people of
all proclivities are given a warm welcome. This is the kind of place
where you're always guaranteed a laugh, so let your perm down
and go for it! (Or sit in the beer garden and simply exude.)
ⓐ 48 Charles St **ⓣ** (029) 2064 0102 **ⓦ** www.exitclubcardiff.com
ⓛ 21.00–02.00 daily

Glam Very smart club that attracts top DJs and a fashion-conscious crowd. The chic lounge has private booths and a VIP area, which has hosted the likes of Oasis. ⓐ 2 Greyfriars Road ⓣ (029) 2022 9311 ⓦ www.glamnightclub.co.uk ⓛ 22.00–03.00 Thur–Sat, closed Sun–Wed ⓘ Book in advance

Ha! Ha! Bar & Canteen This big, cheery bar is a popular option, serving live music, cheap drinks and many a tasty snackette. ⓐ The Friary Centre, The Friary ⓣ 0845 129 7640 ⓛ 10.00–23.00 Mon–Thur, 10.00–24.00 Fri & Sat, 10.30–22.30 Sun

Henry's Bar Smarter than some of its more spit and sawdust neighbours, this is a pre-theatre venue where you don't have to worry about people hurling bar snacks at you for wearing a tux. Henry's has a pleasant terrace and an open-plan bar that serves a decent selection of booze. ⓐ 8–16 Park Place ⓣ (029) 2022 4672 ⓦ www.henryscafebar.co.uk ⓛ 09.00–23.00 Mon–Thur, 09.00–01.00 Fri & Sat, 12.00–19.00 Sun

Live Lounge Live music seven nights a week from a wide range of bands that mainly do covers. ⓐ 9 The Friary ⓦ www.theliveloungecardiff.co.uk ⓛ 17.00–04.00 daily

Mordaith Bar & Grill Posh with a capital P, this upmarket bar-restaurant in a listed building opposite the New Theatre has different areas themed by glamorous international locations. The style is contemporary chic, the menu international and the pre-theatre deals a hit. ⓐ Greyfriars Road ⓣ (029) 2023 3833 ⓛ 11.00–23.00 Sun–Wed, 11.00–03.00 Thur–Sat

Pen & Wig A Cathays classic, this oak-panelled pub exudes come-hither charm. Snuggle up in a leather armchair by the fire or cool down with a pint in the walled beer garden. Please note: the name of the pub does not represent a summary of the dress code. ⓐ 1 Park Grove ⓣ (029) 2064 9090 ⓛ 10.00–24.00 Mon–Fri, 10.00–01.00 Sat, 12.00–23.30 Sun

TigerTiger A night out at this ultra-chic bar and club is a treat for the senses – from mosaics and wood screens in the Medina to minimalist chic in the Tiger Bar and mirrored columns in the club upstairs. Sip creative cocktails, snack on tasty bar food and mingle with Cardiff's cool crowd. ⓐ The Friary ⓣ (029) 2039 1944 ⓦ www.tigertiger-cardiff.co.uk ⓛ 12.00–02.00 Mon–Sat, 12.00–00.30 Sun

Varsity Popular with sports fans for its 12 screens, this large chain pub also has resident DJs on Friday and Saturday as well as karaoke on Sunday. ⓐ Greyfriars Road ⓣ (029) 2023 2562 ⓦ www.varsitybars.com ⓛ 09.00–01.00 Mon–Fri, 09.00–02.00 Sat, 12.00–00.30 Sun

● *The sandy beach at Ogmore-by-Sea on the Glamorgan Heritage Coast*

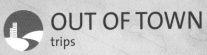

OUT OF TOWN
trips

Glamorgan Heritage Coast

Stretching from Aberthaw to Porthcawl, the 23-km (14-mile) Glamorgan Heritage Coast beckons with secluded coves, clear waters and craggy cliffs. Whether you want to walk golden dunes, grab a wetsuit to hit the surf or climb Celtic castles, this compact coastline in South Wales is wild and wonderful. Two legs or two wheels and you're off!

GETTING THERE

The Glamorgan Heritage Coast is easy to access by public transport. Penarth is just a 20-minute bus ride from central Cardiff (Bus 92), and **Arriva Trains** (❶ 08457 48 49 50 Ⓦ www.arrivatrainswales.co.uk) operates a good service from Cardiff Central Station (see page 48) to Barry Island, Penarth and Bridgend via Llantwit Major. Other useful bus routes include the X2 from Cardiff to Porthcawl via Bridgend and the X91 from Cardiff to Llantwit Major. If you're driving, look out for junctions 33 to 37 on the M4 motorway.

SIGHTS & ATTRACTIONS

Bryngarw Country Park

The mighty oaks and mossy wetlands of this 46-hectare (113-acre) reserve lie just north of Bridgend. Colour-coded trails weave through countryside dotted with lakes and rivers. Relax by the magnolias and maples in the oriental garden, or spot buzzards and woodpeckers. ⓐ Brynmenyn, near Bridgend ❶ (01656) 725155 🕐 10.00–20.00 daily (Apr–Sept); 10.00–18.00 daily (Oct); 10.00–17.00 daily (Nov–Mar)

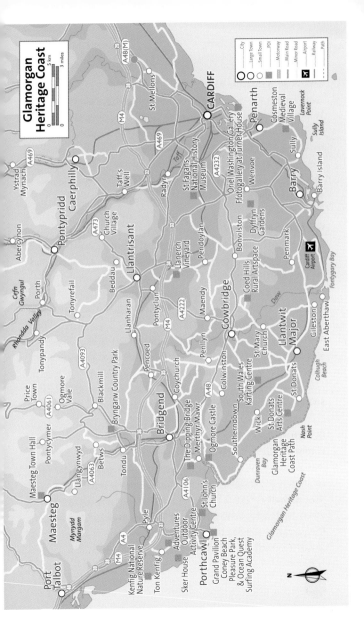

Coney Beach Pleasure Park

Twist and turn to your heart's content on Porthcawl's seafront. Thrill-seekers should make a beeline for the Megablitz roller coaster. You won't find much of the showbiz of state-of-the-art theme parks, but you'll find good, honest fun and you won't grow old in the queues. ⓐ Eastern Promenade, Porthcawl ❶ (01656) 788911 ⓦ www.coneybeach.com ⏰ 15.00–22.00 daily (times depend on weather, so check in advance)

Cosmeston Medieval Village

Stepping back in time to the Middle Ages, this reconstructed 14th-century village offers tours with costumed villagers. ⓐ Country Park, Penarth ❶ (029) 2070 1678 ⏰ 11.00–17.00 daily (summer); 11.00–16.00 daily (winter) ❶ Admission charge

The Dipping Bridge

Spy the holes in the parapets at this 15th-century bridge, where shepherds once pushed their sheep into the River Ogmore to give them a 'dip'. The bridge also has a sinister side: the New Inn that once stood here was home to a landlord who murdered pilgrims en route to St David's shrine. ⓐ Merthyr Mawr ❶ (01656) 815332

Dyffryn Gardens

Cardiff and surrounding districts have got a few surprises up their green sleeves, and this Grade-I-listed Edwardian garden is one of them. Bury your head in fragrant rhododendrons and roses, stroll the vine walk or take in the Victorian ferns and lavender court in the 22-hectare (55-acre) grounds. ⓐ St Nicholas ❶ (029) 2059 3328 ⓦ www.dyffryngardens.org.uk ⏰ 10.00–18.00 daily (summer); 10.00–16.00 daily (winter) ❶ Admission charge

Glamorgan Heritage Coast Path

Explore the hidden nooks of the 23-km (14-mile) Heritage Coast on foot. A trail hugs the length of the coast, from East Aberthaw to Merthyr Mawr's dunes. En route you'll see jagged rocks and sandy bays, Norman castles and Celtic hill settlements. Keep to the cliff paths and watch out for changing tides.

Kenfig National Nature Reserve

This reserve shelters a huge dune system that once spanned Wales's entire south coast. Enjoy sweeping coastal views or explore the area

○ *Taking a dip at The Dipping Bridge*

on an 11-km (7-mile) circular walk via Kenfig Castle and Sker House. The excellent visitor centre offers more information. ⓐ Ton Kenfig, Pyle ⓣ (01656) 743386 ⓦ www.kenfig.org.uk ⓛ 09.00–16.30 Mon–Fri, closed Sat & Sun

Llanerch Vineyard

Taste the grape at Wales's largest vineyard, producing award-winning Cariad wines. Round off your self-guided tour of the vineyard with a tasting of elderflower-tinged whites and fruity rosés. ⓐ Hensol, Pendoylan ⓣ (01443) 225877 ⓦ www.llanerch-vineyard.co.uk ⓛ 10.00–18.00 daily ⓘ Admission charge

Merthyr Mawr

Thatched cottages cluster around the green of this idyllic village. Surrounded by woodlands and meadows, it's the perfect spot for a lazy picnic. Glimpse the eerie remains of Candleston Castle, all that is left of an estate that vanished beneath the sands. ⓣ (01656) 815332

Ogmore Castle

Explore the remains of this enchanting Norman stone-built castle beside the River Ewenny. Skip over the 52 stepping stones crossing the river to Merthyr Mawr, but check tide times first so you don't get stranded. ⓐ Ogmore ⓣ (01656) 815332

Sker House

Sker House is said to be one of Wales's most haunted buildings. It plays the part with aplomb, with its forbidding exterior and one-time monastery credentials. A certain Elizabeth Williams, aka The Maid of Sker, was once imprisoned in the Grade-I-listed manor. Her crime? Susceptibility to the charms of a wandering minstrel. Apparently, her ghost can sometimes be seen hovering about at the window. The house is not currently open to the public, but it's definitely one for your holiday snaps. ❷ Near Porthcawl

Southerndown (Dunraven Bay)

Smooth sands and lofty limestone cliffs make this one of the Heritage Coast's most scenic spots. To the east is Witches' Point and to the west the Ogmore Deeps. Before setting off in search of fossils, check the tides at the visitor centre. ❶ Glamorgan Heritage Coast Centre (01656) 880157

▲ *Mountaineering sheep at Ogmore Castle*

St John's Church

Originally a fortress, Newton's limestone church dates back to the 12th century. The hidden gem here is St John's Well. In the Middle Ages superstitious locals believed that the well possessed magical properties, as it was mysteriously full when the tide was low and empty when it was high. ⓐ Newton

CULTURE

Coed Hills Rural Artspace

Art meets the environment at this eco-friendly gallery. Walk the woodland sculpture trail or learn more about straw-bale building and solar water heating. ⓐ St Hilary, Cowbridge ⓣ (01446) 774084 ⓦ www.coedhills.co.uk ⓛ 10.00–dusk daily

Ffotogallery at Turner House

It's free to admire the photography at this little gem of a gallery in Penarth, an extension of the National Museum Cardiff. ⓐ Plymouth Road, Penarth ⓣ (029) 2070 8870 ⓦ www.ffotogallery.org ⓛ 11.00–17.00 Tues–Sat, closed Sun & Mon

Grand Pavilion

The domed theatre on Porthcawl's seafront stages a variety of festivals, comedy, musical theatre and children's shows. ⓐ The Esplanade, Porthcawl ⓣ (01656) 815995 ⓦ www.grandpavilion.co.uk

Maesteg Town Hall

Maesteg's striking grey-and-red-stone town hall houses a theatre presenting concerts and drama, plus exhibitions including paintings by Welsh artist Christopher Williams. ⓐ Talbot St, Maesteg

(01656) 733269 ⓦ www.maestegtownhall.com ⓛ Variable according to event, so phone to check

Oriel Washington Gallery

Fresh-faced and original, this gallery showcases contemporary Welsh art by the sea. It's also a good place to pick up local craft items such as pottery and handmade jewellery. ⓐ Stanwell Road, Penarth ⓣ (029) 2071 2100 ⓦ www.washingtongallery.co.uk ⓛ 09.00–18.00 Mon–Sat, 10.00–17.30 Sun (summer); 11.00–17.00 Sun (winter)

⬥ The seafront and Grand Pavilion at Porthcawl

GETTING ACTIVE

Maybe it's the rugged coastal profile and the bracing wind, or maybe it's all the iron in the laverbread-and-cockle breakfasts. There's definitely something about this part of the world that transforms mild-mannered holidaymakers into adventurous thrill-seekers. Luckily, there are outlets for your energy dotted up and down the coast.

Thanks to the **Adventures Outdoor Activity Centre** (ⓐ Kenfig, Porthcawl ⓘ (01656) 782300 ⓦ www.adventureswales.co.uk), you can credibly waft into your hotel lobby and trill, 'Gorge scrambling or quad biking, anyone?' This is the place for the ultimate rush, with activities from rock climbing and mountain biking to canoeing and hiking. Or, if you want to burn some rubber, get in pole position at **South Wales Karting Centre** (ⓐ Llandow, near Cowbridge ⓘ (01446) 795568 ⓦ www.swkc.co.uk), an outdoor karting track where life starts

St Donats Arts Centre

A medieval barn converted into a state-of-the-art theatre, this venue lures culture vultures with everything from live jazz and classical concerts to art-house cinema and comedy. ⓐ St Donats ⓘ (01446) 799100 ⓦ www.stdonats.com

RETAIL THERAPY

Bridgend Designer Outlet Village Bag a bargain on designer labels at this outlet village, where 100 shops offer up to a 50 per cent discount on top brands from Karen Millen to Calvin Klein. There's

off in the fast lane and then speeds up – the sensation is the closest you'll get to Formula One racing.

To make sure that those boardshorts don't remain a mere impulse purchase, follow the 'Learn to Surf' sign to learn how to balance on a board at **Cressey's Surf Academy** (☎ (07502) 124030 ⓦ www.cresseyssurfacademy.com). Here the set text is the surfing A–Z, and the learning environment is Coney Beach or Southerndown. For a broader range of watersports that make the most of Porthcawl's waves, try **Ocean Quest** (ⓔ Porthcawl ☎ (01656) 783310 ⓦ www.ocean-quest.co.uk), a top choice for scuba diving, surfing, wakeboarding and kayaking. Take a course with trained professionals or hire equipment and hit the water. And if you don't want to do any surfing but kind of fancy looking like a dude/dudette, the shop here is a veritable boutique of slacker wear.

also a food court, nine-screen cinema, a play area and wheelchair-hire facilities. ⓔ The Derwen, Bridgend ☎ (01656) 665700 ⓦ www.bridgenddesigneroutlet.com ⓛ 10.00–20.00 Mon–Fri, 10.00–19.00 Sat, 10.00–17.00 Sun

Ewenny Pottery It's a pleasure to potter around this craft centre, where Alun Jenkins and family are whizzes on the wheel. The workshop stocks quality hand-thrown glazed earthenware made from local red clay. ⓔ Ewenny ☎ (01656) 653020 ⓦ www.ewennypottery.com ⓛ 09.30–13.00, 14.00–17.00 Mon–Sat, closed Sun

Rhiw Shopping Centre Wall-to-wall high-street shops cluster under one roof. The indoor market is the place to sniff out local produce. ⓐ Bridgend ⓣ (01656) 658704 ⓦ www.rhiwshopping.com ⓛ 08.00–18.00 Mon–Sat, 10.00–16.00 Sun

TAKING A BREAK

Angel Inn £ Conveniently located for Kenfig National Nature Reserve, this cosy 13th-century village pub serves generous lunches. Hearty specials include home-made steak-and-ale pie. The food is good and prices very reasonable. ⓐ Marlas Road, Mawdlam, near Pyle ⓣ (01656) 740456 ⓛ 11.30–23.00 Mon–Sat, closed Sun

Franklin's Café Bar £ Breakfast, sandwiches and home-cooked staples like fisherman's pie are the order of the day in this bright and breezy café. Sip a local beer on the terrace while you admire the view over Hardy's Bay. ⓐ 87 Main Road, Ogmore-by-Sea ⓣ (01656) 880661 ⓦ www.franklinscafébar.co.uk ⓛ 09.00–15.00 Sun, Mon & Wed, 09.00–19.00 Tues, 09.00–21.00 Thur–Sat

Plough and Harrow £ A pit stop on the 8-km (5-mile) circular Nash Point to Monknash walk, this traditional pub is a top choice for lunch and a pint of real ale. ⓐ Monknash, near Llantwit Major ⓣ (01656) 890209 ⓦ www.theploughmonknash.com ⓛ Serves food 12.00–14.30, 18.00–21.00 Mon–Fri, 12.00–17.00, 18.00–20.30 Sat, 12.00–17.00 Sun

AFTER DARK

Blue Anchor Inn £ A favourite among locals, this atmospheric pub with its thatched roof and stone walls dates back to 1380. Pull up a chair by the fire to drink a pint of Brains Bitter. ❷ East Aberthaw ❶ (01446) 750329 Ⓦ www.blueanchoraberthaw.com ❹ Serves food 12.00–14.00, 18.00–20.00 Mon–Thur & Sat, 12.00–14.00 Fri, 12.30–14.30 Sun

The Bear Hotel £–££ This 12th-century hotel and restaurant in Cowbridge serves a slice of history with its home-cooked food and real ales. Enjoy a drink by the fire in the lounge, or venture to the stone-vaulted cellar for à la carte cuisine after dark. ❷ 63 High St, Cowbridge ❶ (01446) 774814 Ⓦ www.bearhotel.com ❹ 12.00–14.30, 18.00–21.30 daily

Frolics Restaurant ££ The imaginative French menu at this Southerndown restaurant features fresh, unfussy dishes like smoked haddock risotto, plus a decent choice of wines. The cliff-top location gives great views over the Bristol Channel. ❷ Beach Road, Southerndown ❶ (01656) 880127 ❹ 12.00–14.30, 18.30–22.00 Wed–Sat, 12.00–14.30 Sun, closed Mon & Tues

Mediterraneo at the Boat House ££ A converted boathouse on Penarth seafront, this inviting Italian restaurant hits the spot with an alfresco aperitif on the terrace, followed by well-cooked seafood, pasta or risotto. ❷ 10 The Esplanade, Penarth ❶ (029) 2070 3428 Ⓦ www.mediterraneopenarth.com ❹ 12.00–22.30 daily

The Olive Tree ££ Expect fresh Welsh fare with a French twist and efficient service at this little restaurant in Penarth. Savour specialities like Glamorgan sausages served with a Roquefort cream sauce. ❷ 21 Glebe St, Penarth ❶ (029) 2070 7077 Ⓦ www.the-olive-tree.net ❹ 17.30–21.00 Tues–Sat, 12.00–14.30 Sun, closed Mon

ACCOMMODATION

Acorn Camping & Caravan Site £ Camp on the coast at this tranquil site in Llantwit Major, set in open farmland near the beach. The facilities include free hot showers, a shop, playground, laundry and games room. **ⓐ** Ham Lane South, Llantwit Major **ⓣ** (01446) 794024 **ⓦ** www.acorncamping.co.uk

Blue Seas Bed & Breakfast Guest House £ Right on the water's edge, this family-run B&B overlooking Newton's beach is a sound choice. Modern single and twin rooms have washbasins and tea-making facilities. **ⓐ** 72 Beach Road, Newton **ⓣ** (01656) 786540 **ⓦ** www.blueseasbnb.co.uk

Best Western Heronston Hotel & Leisure Club ££ Every box is ticked on the basics front at this smart hotel. It's such extras as the sauna, spa pool, gym and steam room that really make the joint stick out, especially at the end of a long day yomping around the coast. **ⓐ** Ewenny Road, Bridgend **ⓣ** (01656) 668811 **ⓦ** www.bw-heronstonhotel.co.uk

Edmon Guest House ££ This smart, well-kept town house in Porthcawl is just a few steps from the beach. En-suite rooms are clean, bright and comfortable. Family rooms also available. **ⓐ** 33 Esplanade Av, Porthcawl **ⓣ** (01656) 788102 **ⓦ** www.edmonguesthouse.co.uk

Great House Hotel ££ Five hundred years old and still looking exquisite, this lovely old hunting lodge sits in gorgeous surroundings and is just the place for showing yourself a good time without

breaking the bank in the process. ❸ High St, Laleston, Bridgend
❶ (01656) 657644 Ⓦ www.great-house-laleston.co.uk

The Old Barn B&B ££ Nature lovers find respite at this beautifully
converted 17th-century barn. Oozing country charm, the guest
house has a peaceful garden overlooking the Vale of Glamorgan.
Comfortable rooms with oak beams and slate floors have all
mod cons. ❸ The Croft, Penmark ❶ (01446) 711352
Ⓦ www.theoldbarnbedandbreakfast.co.uk

Bryngarw House £££ Set in a country park near Bridgend, this
manor house combines 18th-century charm with modern creature
comforts in the 19 en-suite rooms. Dine at The Harlequin restaurant,
or walk one of the trails leading to valleys and hilltops. ❸ Bryngarw
Country Park, Brynmenyn, near Bridgend ❶ (01656) 729009
Ⓦ www.bryngarwhouse.co.uk

Crossways Manor House £££ Surrounded by 24 hectares (6 acres)
of grounds, this greystone mansion has bags of character and is
surprisingly affordable. Details like the central cupola, winding
oak staircase and brass chandeliers add to the charm. Elegant
rooms are bright and spacious, and the Welsh breakfast
substantial. ❸ Cowbridge ❶ (01446) 773171
Ⓦ www.crosswayshouse.co.uk

West House Country Hotel £££ Lovely country house hotel that
dates back to the 17th century. There are 20 stylish bedrooms, some
with four-poster beds, and a Welsh-influenced menu in the
traditional restaurant. ❸ West St, Llantwit Major ❶ (01446) 792406
Ⓦ www.westhouse-hotel.co.uk

The Gower Peninsula & Swansea Bay

The first place in Britain to be designated an area of outstanding natural beauty, the Gower Peninsula has earnt its title. An hour's drive to the west of Cardiff, this 31-km (19-mile) stretch of unspoilt coast, moors and heathland is where the Bristol Channel meets the wild Atlantic. And it's the sea that has shaped the sheltered coves and sandy beaches studding the coastline. From Palaeolithic caves to romantic ruins and Iron Age forts to prehistoric standing stones, the peninsula is a heady mix of coast and culture.

GETTING THERE

An hour's train or bus ride from Cardiff Central Station takes you to Swansea, the gateway to the Gower Peninsula. If you're driving, take the M4 and exit at junction 42 for Swansea Bay, or junction 47 for north Gower. The Gower Explorer Bus makes getting around Gower easy for those without a car. Buses from Swansea shuttle visitors to four walking routes. **Swansea Tourist Information Centre** (❶ (01792) 468321 ❾ www.visitswanseabay.com) offers more details.

SIGHTS & ATTRACTIONS

Arthur's Stone

This monster of a rock has an impressive history to match its size. A Neolithic burial chamber dubbed Arthur's Stone, or Maen Ceti, the boulder measures 4 m (13 ft) high and 2 m (6.5 ft) both wide and deep, and dates back to 2500 BC. Steeped in legend, the mysterious megalith has been associated with King Arthur and St David.
❷ Cefn Bryn

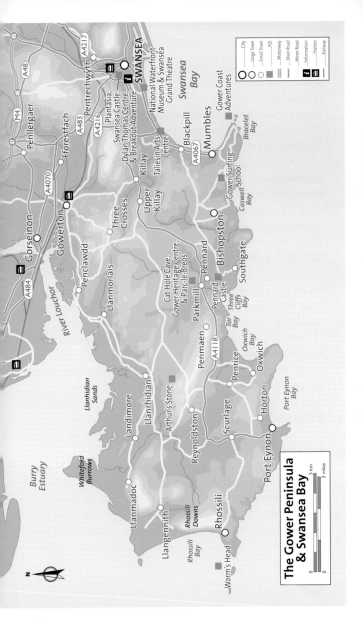

The Gower Peninsula & Swansea Bay

Bracelet Bay

Clean waters wash over the smooth limestone pebbles on this pretty bay, awarded a Blue Flag for cleanliness. Explore the rock pools, spot the white lighthouse guarding the headland or take a ten-minute stroll to Mumbles.

Cat Hole Cave

Follow the footpath from the Gower Heritage Centre through ancient ash woodlands to reach this Stone Age cave. The chambers were used by hunters at the end of the last Ice Age and as a burial site during the Bronze Age. Nearby is Giant's Grave, an important Neolithic burial chamber. 🅐 Parkmill

Gower Coast Adventures

Skim Gower's coastline on the Sea Serpent, with a high-speed round trip to Three Cliffs Bay or Worm's Head. If you're lucky, you'll spy Atlantic Grey Seals and puffins around the rocks. 🅐 Knab Rock, Mumbles ☎ (07866) 250440 🅦 www.gowercoastadventures.co.uk

Mumbles

This quintessential Victorian seaside resort is the perfect tonic after a sightseeing overdose in Cardiff and Swansea. Potter around the boutiques, galleries and craft shops, pausing for an ice cream or coffee by the water's edge. The 244-m (800-ft) pier and medieval Oystermouth Castle are highlights of a visit. ☎ (01792) 361302 🅦 www.mumblestic.co.uk

Oxwich Bay

Mighty dunes and tall cliffs add to the appeal of Oxwich Bay. Three km (2 miles) of clean sands and safe waters make the beach a top choice for families. Watersport enthusiasts catch the surf, while keen walkers follow the coast at low tide to Tor Bay and Three Cliffs Bay. A nature trail from the car park leads to the dunes, taking in the freshwater marshes, woodlands and coastal views.

Pennard Castle

Clinging to the cliff top and perched high above the Pennard Pill stream, this 12th-century castle's crumbling greystone towers afford giddy views of Three Cliffs Bay and Penmaen Burrows. A boardwalk and sandy paths lead down to the beach. ⓐ Pennard

Plantasia

Split into tropical, arid and humid climates, this giant glass pyramid in Swansea shelters rare and endangered species in its glasshouse, aquarium and vivarium. See cacti, cocoa trees and brightly coloured butterflies, or super-sized Giant African Snails. ⓐ Parc Tawe, Swansea ⓘ (01792) 474555 ⓛ 10.00–17.00 daily ⓘ Admission charge

● *Mumbles is a lovely traditional seaside resort, complete with pier*

Rhossili Bay

A smooth, horseshoe-shaped bay backed by the Rhossili Downs, this beautiful spot is a magnet for surfers. For the best views, climb 200 m (656 ft) to the Rhossili Down Commons to spy the 5-km (3-mile) bay and Worm's Head promontory. Beware of undertows if you decide to take a dip here. ❸ National Trust Visitor Centre, Rhossili ❶ (01792) 390707 ● 10.30–17.00 daily

Swansea Castle

Somewhat dwarfed by the modern BT Tower next to it, this was originally a Norman castle overlooking the River Tawe. During Victorian times parts of the castle were used as a prison and town hall. Located in Swansea centre, the castle now stands testimony to the city that has sprung up around it. ❸ Castle Square, Swansea

Three Cliffs Bay

This bay is as scenic as they come, with a sweep of golden sand, thrashed by clear waters and three triangular cliffs rising dramatically above the shore. Spectacular views make it a climbing hotspot, but you can appreciate them on a gentle hike from Penmaen's sand dunes or Parkmill. If you walk beneath the cliffs, make sure you can get back – both the vista and the rip tides can be breathtaking!

Worm's Head

A National Trust Nature Reserve, this serpentine outcrop sits at the westernmost tip of the Gower Peninsula. While it's possible to walk the length of the 'worm', beware of the tides. Atlantic swells show no mercy towards foolhardy tourists, so if you want to play it safe and

⬤ *Beautiful Rhossili Bay is great for surfing*

GETTING ACTIVE

Whether your heart's set on dangling from a rope, wobbling on a board or hurtling along astride a (hopefully) trusty steed, the Gower Peninsula is awash with adrenalin-triggering pursuits. **Breakout Adventure** (ⓐ 26 Woodland Av, Swansea ⓣ (01792) 406023 ⓦ www.breakout-adventure.org) offers no small amount of thrills and spills, with activities ranging from canoeing to caving, coasteering and kayaking.

If you want to ride Wales's waves, **Gower Surfing School** (ⓣ (01792) 360370 ⓦ www.surfgsd.com), Swansea's 4-star approved British Surfing School, is ideal. The centre offers courses for absolute beginners and advanced surfers, and equipment is provided.

At **Parc-le-Breos** (ⓐ Parc-le-Breos House, Parkmill ⓣ (01792) 371636 ⓦ www.parc-le-breos.co.uk) you can gallop along Gower with a professional guide. This riding centre in Parkmill offers half-day and day rides, as well as weekend and week treks. Sturdy footwear and warm clothes are recommended.

avoid getting stranded, soak up the views from Rhossili Bay. ⓐ National Trust Visitor Centre, Rhossili ⓣ (01792) 390707 ⓛ 10.30–17.00 daily

CULTURE

Dylan Thomas Centre

Poetic souls are in their element at this centre dedicated to Swansea's literary hero Dylan Thomas. Located on Swansea's regenerated waterfront, the main exhibition captures the poet's life and work with

murals, readings and video screenings. ❸ Somerset Place, Swansea
❶ (01792) 463980 Ⓦ www.swansea.gov.uk 🕒 10.00–16.30 daily

Gower Heritage Centre

Set around a 12th-century watermill, the centre houses a rural-life
museum and provides guided tours through the corn and saw mill.
A must for families, there are playgrounds, puppet shows and animals.
❸ Parkmill ❶ (01792) 371206 Ⓦ www.gowerheritagecentre.co.uk
🕒 10.00–17.00 daily ❶ Admission charge

National Waterfront Museum

A landmark in Swansea's maritime quarter, this slate-and-glass
structure houses a world-class museum, with interactive exhibits
bringing Wales's industrial past to life. High-tech displays evoke the
Industrial Revolution, from the grime to the gold. Visitors experience
15 themes, including work, landscape, coal and money. See the kinetic
sculptures and virtual shop. ❷ Maritime Quarter, Swansea ❶ (01792)
638950 Ⓦ www.waterfrontmuseum.co.uk 🕒 10.00–17.00 daily

Swansea Grand Theatre

With the grace and grandeur of yesteryear, Swansea's Victorian
theatre is home to the Ballet Russe, the UK's only Russian ballet
company. The huge auditorium stages performances from musicals
and modern dance to stand-up comedy and opera. ❸ Singleton St
❶ (01792) 475715 Ⓦ www.swanseagrand.co.uk

Taliesin Arts Centre

Venture into Swansea's lesser-known cultural waters at this arts
centre, part of the city's university. Independent films, innovative
productions, contemporary art and Wales's largest collection of

Egyptian artefacts make this a good choice. ⓐ Swansea University, Singleton Park ⓣ (01792) 602060 ⓦ www.taliesinartscentre.co.uk

RETAIL THERAPY

Lovespoon Gallery Buy a hand-carved Welsh lovespoon in the Mumbles. Patricia Price's traditional tokens of affection are carved from a single piece of wood, with over 300 designs to choose from. ⓐ 492 Mumbles Road ⓣ (01792) 360132 ⓦ www.lovespoons.co.uk ⓛ 10.00–17.30 Mon–Sat, closed Sun

Mumbles Fine Wines No grape is left untrodden at this emporium that's in the *vin*-guard of the area's burgeoning wine scene. Not only can you acquire a decent bottle of plonk, but there are also courses, tastings and a nice line in French deli fare. ⓐ 524 Mumbles Road ⓣ (01792) 367663 ⓦ www.mumblesfinewines.co.uk ⓛ 10.00–20.00 Mon–Sat, 11.00–17.00 Sun

Oyster Gallery Enjoy coastal living at home with a nautical-themed accessory or photo from this stylish gallery-cum-home décor shop. There are also paintings by local artists. ⓐ 70–72 Newton Road, Mumbles ⓣ (01792) 366988 ⓦ www.oystergallery.co.uk ⓛ 09.00–17.30 Mon–Sat, 11.00–16.00 Sun

PJ's Surf Shop Want to tackle those waves? Kit yourself out with a board, wetsuit and a set of fins from this Llangennith shop. ⓐ Llangennith ⓣ (01792) 386669 ⓦ www.pjsurfshop.co.uk ⓛ 09.30–17.30 daily

Swansea Market Fresh cockles, laverbread and organic fruits fill the stalls at central Swansea's covered market, the largest of its

kind in Wales. This is a buzzing spot to shop for local produce and crafts under one roof. ❸ Oxford Street, Swansea
❶ (01792) 654296 ❾ www.swanseaindoormarket.co.uk
❶ 08.00–17.30 Mon–Sat, closed Sun

TAKING A BREAK

Bay Bistro & Coffee House £ This cosy bistro and café in Rhossili serves snacks and light lunches such as jacket potatoes, panini and home-made shepherd's pie. ❸ Rhossili ❶ (01792) 390519 ❶ 10.00–17.30, 19.00–21.00 daily

Café Twocann £ Popular café in a Grade-II-listed former docks building on Swansea's redeveloped waterfront. ❸ Unit 2, J Shed, King's Road, Swansea ❶ (01792) 458000 ❾ www.cafetwocann.com
❶ 11.00–16.00 Mon–Thur, 10.00–16.00 Sat & Sun, Fri & Sat eves

Surfside Café £ The perfect pit stop for a coffee, panini or real dairy ice cream, this chain of chilled cafés has great sea views. ❸ Caswell Bay, Langland and Rotherslade ❶ (01792) 368368 ❶ 09.00–17.30 daily

▲ *Treat yourself to tea and cakes in one of Mumbles's many cafés*

Three Cliffs Coffee Shop £ Open 364 days a year, this café near Three Cliffs Bay serves light meals using Welsh produce, plus cakes and hot drinks. ⓐ 68 Southgate Road, Southgate ⓣ (01792) 233230 ⓦ www.threecliffs.com ⓛ 09.00–18.00 daily

Verdi's Café & Ice Cream Parlour £ Pause for a cappuccino, pizza or one of 30 varieties of fresh ice cream at this excellent Italian café on the Mumbles seafront. ⓐ Knab Rock, Mumbles ⓣ (01792) 369135 ⓦ www.verdis-cafe.co.uk ⓛ 10.00–21.30 daily

The Welcome to Town Country Bistro ££ Opposite the village church in Llanrhidian, this charming 17th-century cottage serves well-prepared Welsh fare. Feast on a lunch of laverbread and black beef beneath the beams. ⓐ Llanrhidian ⓣ (01792) 390015 ⓦ www.thewelcometotown.co.uk ⓛ 12.00–14.00, 19.00–21.30 Tues–Sat, 12.00–14.00 Sun, closed Mon

AFTER DARK

Bay View Bar £ Swansea Bay meets Siam at this bar serving Thai food fresh from the wok. Come here for lunch, dinner or to relax with a drink by the open fire. ⓐ 400 Oystermouth Road, Swansea ⓣ (01792) 652610 ⓦ www.bayviewbar.co.uk ⓛ 12.00–15.00, 18.00–22.00 Mon–Sat, 12.00–15.00, 18.00–21.00 Sun

Café Valance £ A fashionable and busy café-bar with attractive outdoor terraces that serves pizzas, salads and burgers. Don't leave without trying one of their famous cappuccinos. ⓐ 50 Newton Road, Mumbles ⓣ (01792) 367711 ⓦ www.cafevalance.com ⓛ 09.00–21.00 Mon–Sat, 10.00–17.00 Sun

Truffle £ The set three-course menu at this North-African-inspired restaurant offers great value. You can bring a bottle and there's no corkage fee. ⓐ 68 Brynymor Road, Swansea ⓣ (01792) 547246 ⓦ www.truffle-swansea.co.uk ⓛ 18.30–23.00 Wed–Sat, closed Sun–Tues

Bouchon de Rossi ££ Laid-back and friendly, this French café and bistro scores points for its eclectic menu and efficient staff. Try the garlicky mussels or beer-battered cod. ⓐ 217 Oxford St, Swansea ⓣ (01792) 655780 ⓦ www.bouchonderossi.co.uk ⓛ 12.00–14.30, 18.00–21.30 Tues–Sat, closed Sun & Mon

Hanson at the Chelsea Restaurant ££ Head to Swansea's café quarter for this hip place, with its clean colours, wooden floors and original art. Head chef Andrew Hanson uses organic, local produce such as fresh cockles and Gower lamb. ⓐ 17 St Mary's St, Swansea ⓣ (01792) 464068 ⓦ www.thechelseacafe.co.uk ⓛ 12.00–14.00, 18.30–21.30 Tues–Sat, closed Sun & Mon

Fairyhill Hotel & Restaurant £££ Blow the budget on 5-star cuisine at this vine-clad 18th-century manor set in 10 hectares (24 acres) of grounds. Specialities include seared scallops and filo tart of vine tomatoes with local goat's cheese. ⓐ Reynoldston ⓣ (01792) 390139 ⓦ www.fairyhill.net ⓛ 12.00–14.00, 19.00–21.00 daily

ACCOMMODATION

Bank Farm Leisure Park £ A few steps from the beach, this 30-hectare (75-acre) campsite has views of Port Eynon Bay. Plus points include

the on-site bar, heated outdoor pool, children's playground and grocery shop. ❷ Bank Farm Leisure Park, Horton ❶ (01792) 390228 ❾ www.bankfarmleisure.co.uk

Nicholaston Farm Caravan & Camping £ Just off the Swansea to Port Eynon road, this campsite on a working farm has pick-your-own fruit. Spacious pitches on the meadow overlook Tor Bay, and nearby Cefn Bryn hill affords sweeping views over Gower. ❷ Penmaen ❶ (01792) 371209 ❾ www.nicholastonfarm.co.uk

Pitton Cross £ Pitch a tent at this peaceful site with sea views. It's an ideal base for coastal walks to Worm's Head and Rhossili Bay, with clean facilities, a laundry room, shop and play area. ❷ Pitton Cross, Rhossili ❶ (01792) 390593 ❾ www.pittoncross.co.uk

The Coast House ££ This family-run guesthouse on the Mumbles seafront offers good value. Enjoy clean and comfy en-suite rooms, some with views of Swansea Bay. ❷ 708 Mumbles Road ❶ (01792) 368702 ❾ www.thecoasthouse.co.uk

Highmead B&B ££ Coastal walks, sandy beaches and Port Eynon are on the doorstep of this 4-star B&B. All rooms have sea views and there's a lounge where you can unwind after a long hike. ❷ Overton, Port Eynon ❶ (01792) 390300 ❾ www.highmead-gower.co.uk

King Arthur Hotel ££ Legend has it that this is a great place to stay on Gower. The country inn lives up to its reputation, with spotless, spacious rooms overlooking gardens. A bonus is the pub's restaurant serving hearty Welsh food and real ales. ❷ Higher Green, Reynoldston ❶ (01792) 390775 ❾ www.kingarthurhotel.co.uk

Little Haven Guesthouse ££ This first-rate Oxwich B&B has homely en-suite rooms, a heated outdoor pool and a terrace. The beach is just a short stroll away. ⓐ Oxwich Bay ⓣ (01792) 390940 ⓦ www.littlehavenoxwich.co.uk

North Gower Hotel ££ Located in gardens and overlooking the Loughor Estuary, this olde-worlde hotel in Llanrhidian has 18 well-kept rooms with mod cons. There's a good restaurant and bar on-site. ⓐ Llanrhidian ⓣ (01792) 390042 ⓦ www.northgowerhotel.co.uk

Parc-le-Breos ££ You'll feel like lord of the manor at this grand 19th-century hunting lodge in 28 hectares (70 acres) of grounds. A 1.6-km (1-mile) drive through woods and meadows brings you to the lodge, with its log fires, carp pond and terrace. Combine your stay with a canter along the coast. ⓐ Parc-le-Breos House, Parkmill ⓣ (01792) 371636 ⓦ www.parc-le-breos.co.uk

Barlands Cottage £££ A quiet 250-year-old cottage in the Bishopston Valley, this B&B exudes country charm. Snug en-suite rooms decorated in warm colours have a TV and tea-making facilities. ⓐ Old Kittle Road, Bishopston ⓣ (01792) 232615 ⓦ www.barlandscottage.co.uk

The Dragon Hotel £££ For those who prefer retro to rustic, this modern and central Swansea hotel offers affordable indulgence in Zen-style rooms. After hiking or biking Gower, relax with a massage at the health club or cocktails at the bar. ⓐ Kingsway Circle, Swansea ⓣ (01792) 657100 ⓦ www.dragon-hotel.co.uk

Brecon Beacons National Park

Spanning 1,347 sq km (520 sq miles), the Brecon Beacons National Park has a raw beauty and sense of solitude. Above ground, moors and dense woodlands are dominated by limestone crags and lofty peaks. Below ground, chambers, caves and mines interweave. Prime hiking, biking and camping territory just an hour's drive north of Cardiff.

GETTING THERE

While a car makes getting to remote corners of the national park easier, Cardiff has good public transport connections to the main towns. The frequent X43 service (see Ⓦ www.sixtysixty.co.uk) links Cardiff bus station to Merthyr Tydfil, Brecon, Crickhowell and Abergavenny. Arriva Trains (see page 104) runs an hourly service from Cardiff to Merthyr Tydfil and a half-hourly train from Cardiff to Abergavenny.

SIGHTS & ATTRACTIONS

Beacons Horseshoe

If you've got a head for heights, this 14-km (9-mile) hike could appeal. The challenging ridge walk encompasses the Brecon Beacons' three highest peaks: Pen y Fan (886 m/2,907 ft), Corn Du (873 m/2,864 ft) and Cribyn (795 m/2,608 ft). Some parts are steep, but trekkers are rewarded with sweeping views of peaks, lakes and valleys. Allow seven hours (start early), pick up a map and check weather conditions before heading out. ⓐ Cwm Gedi Training Camp car park (off the B4601)

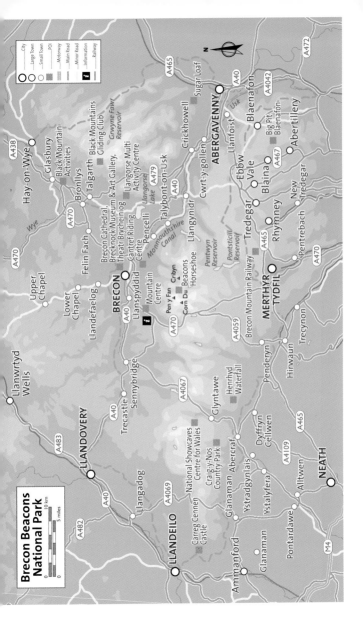

Big Pit Blaenafon

Part of the UNESCO World Heritage Site of Blaenafon, Big Pit offers free underground tours of a real coal mine with visitors descending 90 m (295 ft) down the mineshaft in a pit cage. Don't miss the colliery buildings, mining galleries and Pithead Baths. ⓐ Blaenafon ⓣ (01495) 790311 ⓦ www.museumwales.ac.uk ⓛ 09.30–17.00 daily. Underground tours 10.00–15.30

Brecon Mountain Railway

Too tired to climb every mountain? Let a steam train do the hard work. Enjoy views over the Taf Fechan Reservoir and the Brecon Beacons' trio of peaks. ⓐ Pant Station, Merthyr Tydfil ⓣ (01685) 722988 ⓦ www.breconmountainrailway.co.uk ⓛ 09.30–16.00 Apr–Oct (see website for other times of year) ⓘ Admission charge

Craig-y-Nos Country Park

This peaceful country park in the upper Swansea Valley is a patchwork of lakes, meadows, rivers and forests. Trails weave through the park and it's a great spot for a picnic in summer. ⓐ Brecon Road, Penycae ⓣ (01639) 730395 ⓛ 10.00–dusk daily

Henrhyd Waterfall

Water cascades 27 m (89 ft) at the highest falls in the Brecon Beacons. Tucked away in a green gorge, the striking waterfall can be reached by taking the steep footpath through the woods. ⓐ National Trust car park, near Coelbren (off the A4221)

Llangorse Lake

This nutrient-rich lake is a haven for wildlife, including yellow water lilies and dragonflies. Flanked by reeds and willow woods, the tranquil lake was carved out by glacial movement during the last Ice Age. ❷ Llangorse

Mountain Centre

Eight km (5 miles) southwest of Brecon, this helpful visitor centre has plenty of information, maps, books and an exhibition on the national park. There are great views of Pen y Fan from here and you can recharge your batteries with a light lunch in the café. ❷ Libanus ❶ (01874) 623366 ❿ www.brecon-beacons.com ❹ 09.30–17.00 daily (summer); 09.30–16.30 daily (winter)

⬥ *Let the train take the strain on the Brecon Mountain Railway*

GETTING ACTIVE

Adrenalin-fuelled pursuits are a major draw in the Black Mountains. **Black Mountain Activities** (🅰 Three Cocks, Brecon ☎ (01497) 847897 🆆 www.blackmountain.co.uk) is an organisation that offers outdoor thrills, including rock climbing, high rope courses, gorge walking, caving, potholing and kayaking. Day courses for beginners are available.

Cantref Riding Centre (🅰 Cantref, Brecon ☎ (01874) 665223 🆆 www.cantref.com) is a top address for horse riding in the Brecon Beacons. Treks cater to all levels and include half-day rides to the foothills, plus day rides to the mountains and woodlands. An on-site farmhouse and bunkhouse make this a good base.

🔺 *Kayaking in the Black Mountains*

A holiday is the perfect time to try a new activity so why not explore the national park from a different angle? **Black Mountains Gliding Club** (☎ (01874) 711463 🖥 www.blackmountainsgliding.co.uk) offers trial flights accompanied by an instructor during which you'll be invited to take the controls. You might even be lucky enough to soar alongside a red kite. Those after adventure in high doses will not be disappointed at the multi-award-winning **Llangorse Multi Activity Centre** (🏠 Gilfach Farm, Llangorse ☎ (01874) 658272 🖥 www.activityuk.com). Here you can get wet and muddy dingle scrambling, traversing waterfalls, crawling through pipes or swinging through the treetops. It's also Wales's biggest climbing and riding centre.

If you're feeling particularly energetic, hit the Taff Trail. Linking Brecon to Cardiff Bay, this 89-km (55-mile) trail is a magnet to hikers and mountain bikers. A network of railway, canal and forest paths takes in highlights such as **Castell Coch** (🏠 Castle Hill ☎ (029) 2081 0101), Merthyr Tydfil and the Talybont Reservoir. For details, see 🖥 www.tafftrail.org.uk

National Showcaves Centre for Wales

Lose yourself in an underground labyrinth of chambers, passages and caves at these award-winning caves. Glimpse yawning Cathedral Cave and spooky Bone Cave, where 3,000-year-old skeletons were discovered. The site also features a reconstructed Iron Age village, conservation museum and farm. 🏠 Dan-yr-Ogof ☎ (01639) 730284 🖥 www.showcaves.co.uk 🕐 10.00–15.00 daily (Apr–Oct) ❶ Admission charge

Sugar Loaf

Climb to the narrow ridge of this conical 596-m (1,955-ft) mountain for 360-degree views of the Bristol Channel and Malvern Hills. To the north of Abergavenny, the uphill trek through moors and woodlands begins in the car park that can be reached on a narrow lane just off the A40.

CULTURE

Brecknock Museum & Art Gallery

Housed in a Victorian shire hall, this intriguing museum and art gallery traces local and natural history, with displays on Welsh life, industry and crafts. Highlights include the huge collection of Welsh lovespoons. ⓐ Captain's Walk, Brecon ⓣ (01874) 624121 ⓛ 10.00–17.00 Mon–Fri, 10.00–13.00, 14.00–17.00 Sat, closed Sun (and first Monday of every month)

Brecon Cathedral

Explore 900 years of history at Brecon's beautiful cathedral, dating back to 1094. Admire Britain's largest Norman font before visiting the heritage centre and craft shop in the 16th-century tithe barn. ⓐ Cathedral Close, Brecon ⓣ (01874) 623857 ⓦ www.breconcathedral.org.uk ⓛ 08.30–18.00 daily

Carreg Cennen Castle

Clinging to a limestone crag above the River Cennen, this greystone fortress is worth the climb. The romantic 13th-century castle is one of Wales's most impressive, with giddy views of the Black Mountain. ⓐ Trapp, near Llandeilo ⓣ (01558) 822291 ⓦ www.carregcennencastle.com ⓛ 09.30–18.00 daily (Apr–Sept); 09.30–16.00 daily (Oct–Mar) ⓘ Admission charge

▲ *There's plenty to do and see in the pretty market town of Brecon*

Theatr Brycheiniog

Brecon's modern theatre stages first-rate concerts and performances, welcoming leading companies to the stage such as The Royal National Theatre and BBC National Orchestra of Wales. The eclectic line-up stretches from jazz and rock to musicals, ballet and comedy.

ⓐ Canal Wharf, Brecon ⓣ (01874) 611622 ⓦ www.brycheiniog.co.uk
ⓛ Box office 09.30–17.00 Mon–Sat, closed Sun

RETAIL THERAPY

Beacons Crafts This workshop and studios in central Brecon showcases Welsh arts and crafts, from woodwork to ceramics, jewellery, textiles, candles and glasswork. ⓐ Bethel Square, Brecon ⓣ (01874) 625706
ⓦ www.beaconscrafts.co.uk ⓛ 10.00–17.00 Mon–Sat, closed Sun

Brecon Farmers' Market Fresh local produce fills the stalls at this market held in Brecon on the second Saturday of the month (except August). Shop for organic vegetables, fruit, cheese and chutney to the sound of live jazz or classical music. ⓐ Brecon ⓒ 09.30–14.00 Sat, closed Sun–Fri

Sugar Loaf Vineyards These peaceful vineyards overlooking the Usk Valley offer wine tastings and tours. ⓐ Pentre Lane, Abergavenny ⓣ (01873) 853066 ⓦ www.sugarloafvineyard.co.uk ⓒ 10.30–17.00 Mon–Sat, 12.00–17.00 Sun (Mar–Dec)

TAKING A BREAK

Llanfaes Dairy Ice Cream Bar £ See ice cream being made fresh on the premises at this parlour. Satisfy your sweet tooth with one of 40 flavours, like pink grapefruit, chocolate orange and Turkish delight. ⓐ 19 Bridge St, Brecon ⓣ (01874) 625892 ⓦ www.llanfaesdairy.net ⓒ 10.00–17.30 daily

● *Take a break in a cosy café in Brecon*

The Old Barn Tearoom £ Pause at this atmospheric 18th-century barn to the north of the Taff Valley to try the delicious homemade cakes with a pot of tea. You'll find the tearoom on the mountain road between Talybont-on-Usk and Merthyr Tydfil. ❷ Ystradgynwyn ❶ (01685) 383358 ❸ 11.00–17.00 daily

Pilgrims Tea Rooms £ Beneath Brecon Cathedral's cloisters, you'll find this award-winning gem of a tearoom. Janet Williams serves light lunches and afternoon teas using local ingredients. Enjoy a warming lamb casserole, freshly baked flapjack, or pre-book a picnic hamper for lunch in the hills. ❷ Brecon Cathedral Close ❶ (01874) 610610 ❿ www.pilgrims-tearooms.co.uk ❸ 10.00–17.00 daily (summer); 10.00–16.00 daily (winter)

AFTER DARK

RESTAURANTS

The Crown at Pantygelli £ Welsh black beef is the star of the show on the traditional menu in this pretty country pub. Admire the views from the garden while you sip a locally brewed beer. ❷ Old Hereford Road, Pantygelli, Abergavenny ❶ (01873) 853314 ❿ www.thecrownatpantygelli.com ❸ 12.00–14.30 Tues–Fri, 12.00–15.00 Sat & Sun, 18.00–23.00 Mon–Sat, 18.00–22.30 Sun

The Dragon Inn £ The imaginative menu ranges from Welsh black steaks to mussels in Thai green curry at this 17th-century hotel in Crickhowell. ❷ High St, Crickhowell ❶ (01873) 810362 ❿ www.dragonhotel.co.uk ❸ 12.00–14.00, 18.30–21.30 Mon–Sat, 12.00–14.00 Sun

The White Hart £ If it's cold outside, warm yourself by the log fires in the bar and beamed dining room at this 16th-century coaching inn. Welsh specialities like roast duck with sloe gin are staples on the menu. In summer sample real ales in the beer garden. ❸ Talybont-on-Usk ❶ (01874) 676227 Ⓦ www.breconbunkhouse.co.uk ⏱ 12.00–20.30 Sun–Thur, 12.00–21.00 Fri & Sat

The Felin Fach Griffin £–££ Head chef Ricardo Van Ede won a Michelin star at the age of 21. His foodie philosophy is simple: eat, drink, sleep (and be merry). Expect home-grown vegetables and high-quality local produce like Welsh venison and Portland crab to land on your plate. ❷ Felin Fach ❶ (01874) 620111 Ⓦ www.eatdrinksleep.ltd.uk ⏱ 19.00–21.30 Mon, 12.30–14.30, 19.00–21.30 Tues–Sun

Nantyffin Cider Mill Inn ££ Looking pretty in pink, this award-winning inn at the foot of the Black Mountains is set around a 16th-century cider mill. The characterful restaurant combines fresh flavours like Cornish mussels with cider and leeks. ❸ Brecon Road ❶ (01873) 810775 Ⓦ www.cidermill.co.uk ⏱ 12.00–14.30, 18.30–21.30 Tues–Sun, closed Mon

Roberto's Italian Restaurant ££ An intimate feel and Italian dishes cooked with finesse tempt at this laid-back trattoria in Brecon. It's a pleasant spot for dinner after a long day's sightseeing. Booking is recommended. ❷ The Old Sorting Office, St Mary's St, Brecon ❶ (01874) 611880 ⏱ 17.30–22.00 daily

The Usk Inn ££ A welcome break, this award-winning village inn prides itself on seafood and traditional Welsh fare. Tuck into crab fishcakes, garlicky mussels or Caecrwn pork in the bistro, or kick back with a

pint of real ale on the terrace. ❸ Talybont-on-Usk ❶ (01874) 676251
🌐 www.uskinn.co.uk 🕒 Restaurant 12.00–14.00, 18.30–21.30 daily

ACCOMMODATION

Anchorage Caravan Park £ Pitch a tent at this leafy family-run
campsite, with panoramic views of the nearby Black Mountains.
Excellent facilities include a shop, post office, laundry room, hair
salon, TV lounge and play area. ❸ Bronllys ❶ (01874) 711246
🌐 www.anchoragecp.co.uk

Canal Barn Bunkhouse £ Popular with hikers and cyclists, this
bunkhouse is 5-star roughing it. Tucked away in rural Trecastle, the
oak-beamed cow shed offers comfy beds, plenty of hot water, and
a communal kitchen and dining room. A bridle path leads to Roman
ruins. Bring your own sleeping bag and towel. ❸ Ynysmarchog Farm,
Trecastle ❶ (01874) 638000 🌐 www.bunkhousewales.co.uk

Lakeside Caravan & Camping Park £ Set in open countryside, this
peaceful site is just a short stroll from Llangorse Lake and is a good
base to explore the Beacons. Guest facilities include a clubhouse,
shop and café. You can hire boats, canoes and windsurfing equipment
here. ❸ Llangorse ❶ (01874) 658226 🌐 www.lakeside-holidays.net
🕒 Apr–Oct

Pencelli Castle £ This multi-award-winning site is set in a tranquil spot
6 km (4 miles) from Brecon. Walk the highest peaks, hire mountain
bikes or launch a canoe on the canal that runs through the meadow.
The site is also a Wi-Fi hotspot. ❸ Pencelli ❶ (01874) 665451
🌐 www.pencelli-castle.co.uk

YHA Brecon £ Not just another bog-standard hostel, this rambling house just a couple of miles outside Brecon has real Victorian charm. First-rate facilities include a barbecue area, common room, cycle store, kitchen and laundry. ⓐ Groesffordd ⓣ 0845 371 9506 ⓦ www.yha.org.uk

Blaencar Farm ££ Escape to the country at this working farm. All exposed beams, stonework and heavy oak doors, the traditional farmhouse serves a hearty breakfast. The friendly owners can help with maps, storage and packed lunches. ⓐ Sennybridge ⓣ (01874) 636610 ⓦ www.blaencar.co.uk

Castle of Brecon Hotel £££ Sitting on Brecon Castle's remains, this whitewashed 18th-century coaching inn rises above the town with superb views of the River Usk Valley. The elegant rooms have TV, coffee-making facilities and direct-dial phone. ⓐ The Castle Square, Brecon ⓣ (01874) 624611 ⓦ www.breconcastle.co.uk

Llwyn Onn Guest House £££ This country house overlooking the Llwyn Onn Reservoir is a good base for the Taff Trail. Smart rooms have views over gardens or woodland and you can use the nearby spa for free. ⓐ Llwyn Onn, near Merthyr Tydfil ⓣ (01685) 384384 ⓦ www.llwynonn.co.uk

Nant Ddu £££ If you're craving creature comforts, this spa retreat is just the ticket. Stylish rooms look out on lawns, fields and forest. Snuggle up by the log fire in the bar or unwind in the hydro-spa and sauna. ⓐ Cwm Taf, near Merthyr Tydfil ⓣ (01685) 379111 ⓦ www.nant-ddu-lodge.co.uk

---

▶ *The clock tower at Cardiff Castle*

PRACTICAL
information

Directory

GETTING THERE
By air

Many international airlines serve Cardiff Airport (see page 48) with direct and frequent flights to major European cities, including Paris, Brussels and Amsterdam, as well as the Caribbean. For budget deals, your best bet is **bmibaby** (📞 0905 8282828 🌐 www.bmibaby.com), operating a frequent service to a number of key European destinations, including Belfast, Glasgow, Faro and Alicante. Other big airlines serving the city include **KLM** (📞 08712 310000 🌐 www.klm.com), **Thomsonfly** (📞 08712 314787 🌐 www.thomsonfly.com), **Aer Lingus** (📞 0871 718 5000 🌐 www.aerlingus.com) and **Flybe** (📞 08444 125959 🌐 www.flybe.com). To compare prices, check out 🌐 www.skyscanner.net. Another option is to fly to nearby Bristol or Birmingham airport and connect from there.

Many people are aware that air travel emits CO_2, which contributes to climate change. You may be interested in the possibility of lessening the environmental impact of your flight through the charity **Climate Care** (🌐 www.jpmorganclimatecare.com), which offsets your CO_2 by funding environmental projects around the world.

By rail

Cardiff Central Station (see page 48) has excellent rail connections to major cities across the UK. **First Great Western** (📞 08457 000125 🌐 www.firstgreatwestern.co.uk) operates an hourly service to London Paddington; the journey takes roughly 2 hours. There are frequent services to other major hubs including Bristol (45 minutes), Swansea (1 hour) and Birmingham (2 hours). **National Rail** (📞 0845 748 4950 🌐 www.nationalrail.co.uk) gives comprehensive information on fares, destinations and timetables.

By road

Travelling by bus is perhaps the cheapest, if slowest, way to reach other UK destinations like London, Bristol, Oxford and Glasgow. **National Express** (☏ 08717 818181 ⓦ www.nationalexpress.com) and **Megabus** (☏ 0900 160 0900 ⓦ www.megabus.com) link Cardiff to London and offer some great deals if you're flexible about when you travel.

The roads and motorways are good and fast through Wales, and with a clear run on the M4 you can drive from London to Cardiff in 2 hours 30 minutes. If possible, it's best to avoid driving during rush hour (08.00–09.30 and 17.00–18.30) when motorways can be congested. It takes around 3 hours and 30 minutes to reach Dover, where there are regular ferries to Calais in France.

ENTRY FORMALITIES

Entry and visa requirements for Wales are the same as for the rest of the UK. EU, US, Canadian, Australian, South African and New Zealand citizens must have a valid passport, but do not need a visa. Visitors from other countries may need a visa to enter the UK and should contact their consulate or embassy before departure. More information on visas is available at ⓦ www.ukvisas.gov.uk

MONEY

The national currency is the British pound (GBP), which is divided into 100 pence. ATM machines are plentiful in the city centre and accept most major credit and debit cards, including Visa and MasterCard. Most restaurants, hotels and department stores accept Visa, MasterCard and American Express. Many shops, especially in areas frequented by tourists, also accept card payments.

HEALTH, SAFETY & CRIME

Wales is generally a safe place to visit and there are no particular health risks. No vaccinations or health certificates are required and the tap water is safe to drink.

Pharmacies stock medication to treat minor ailments. They usually open between 08.30 and 18.00 Monday to Saturday and 11.00 to 17.00 Sunday. Dispensaries at major supermarkets often stay open later.

The British National Health Service (NHS) offers free emergency care to EU citizens and nationals from countries with reciprocal health agreements with the UK, including Australia and New Zealand.

There is a charge for routine medical care. Travellers from other countries such as the USA, Canada and South Africa should invest in a good health insurance policy.

Further information is given on the Department of Health website
Ⓦ www.dh.gov.uk

Cardiff has a low crime rate and travel is generally safe here, even for lone travellers. However, it's advisable to take good care of your belongings and be aware of your surroundings. The general rules apply about not carrying large sums of money, or drawing unwanted attention with expensive jewellery and cameras. If you are the victim of a crime or other emergency, you should inform the police immediately by calling
Ⓣ 999. See Emergencies (page 154) for further details and listings.

OPENING HOURS

Most shops in Cardiff open from 09.00 to 18.00 Monday to Saturday and 11.00 to 17.00 Sunday. Some of the city's shopping centres and department stores open later on Thursdays. The majority of Cardiff's key attractions open from 10.00 to 17.00 daily. Some open later during the summer months. Banks generally open from 09.00 to 17.00 Monday to Saturday, although some smaller branches may close at the weekend.

TOILETS

There are a number of attended public toilets in the city centre that are clean and well maintained, as well as automatic conveniences. You'll find attended toilets at Hayes Island, St David's, Wood Street and Kingsway. Most facilities open between 08.00 and 17.00 daily, and unattended toilets are open 24 hrs.

CHILDREN

A green and child-friendly city, Cardiff appeals to families with its leafy parks, fairy-tale castles and interactive museums. There's plenty to keep children entertained, from playgrounds where they can let off excess energy to safe and sandy beaches on the nearby Glamorgan Heritage Coast (see page 104), where children can paddle or hunt for fossils. Children are welcome in most cafés and restaurants, some offering special menus to suit little appetites. They can play freely on the pirate ships in Cardiff Bay's sandy playground. There is also an adventure playground in Roath Park (see page 62).

When the sun shines, take your children to the seaside. A 20-minute ride from Cardiff, **Barry Island Pleasure Park** (ⓐ Barry Island ⓣ (01446) 732844) opens during the school summer holidays and draws families with its log flume, roller coasters and giant pirate ship. At the National Museum Cardiff (see page 96) children will love the Evolution of Wales, tracing the country's history back millions of years to the age of dinosaurs and woolly mammoths. You can always keep boredom at bay with a visit to the **Red Dragon Centre** (ⓐ Hemingway Road ⓣ (029) 2025 6261 ⓦ www.thereddragoncentre.co.uk), a leisure complex featuring the Doctor Who Exhibition (see page 78), a 12-screen Odeon cinema, 26-lane bowling alley and diner-style restaurants serving children's favourite foods. Children can get to grips with science at Techniquest hands-on discovery museum (see page 80) and test out 160 interactive exhibits, from firing a rocket to launching a hot-air balloon, experimenting in the laboratory or studying stars in the planetarium.

There are nappy-changing facilities in most of Cardiff's major department stores and also in Cardiff Bay's clean public toilets and some attractions, including Techniquest.

⬤ *Children love the statues on the waterfront at Cardiff Bay*

COMMUNICATIONS

Internet

Cardiff has its share of Internet cafés, although things are moving more towards Wi-Fi these days. There are some good, cheap options in the city centre, including the tourist office, where you'll pay around £1 for an hour online. Two reliable options are:

Cardiff Central Library If you want to surf for free, head for this library. Wales's largest public library has over 90 PCs offering high-speed Internet access. There is a small charge for print-outs. ⓐ The Hayes ☏ (029) 2038 2116 ⏰ 09.00–18.00 Mon–Fri, 09.00–17.30 Sat, closed Sun

Talk & Surf A short walk west of the train station, this cybercafé is popular with visitors to the city. ⓐ 62 Tudor St ☏ (029) 2022 6820 ⏰ 09.30–22.00 daily

Phone

BT public telephone boxes are widely available in Cardiff and accept coins (10p, 20p, 50p and £1), phonecards and, occasionally, credit and debit cards. Two useful reference points are:

International UK Directory Enquiries ☏ 118 505
UK Directory Enquiries ☏ 118 500

Post

Stamps are sold in post offices and some newsagents. The postal service in Wales is quick and efficient. There are a number of branches dotted throughout the city, including one in Cowbridge Road East and another in Albany Road. The main post office (ⓐ 45–46 Queens Arcade ☏ 08457 223344 ⓦ www.postoffice.co.uk ⏰ 09.00–17.30 Mon–Sat, closed Sun) also has a bureau de change and shop.

TELEPHONING CARDIFF

To phone Cardiff from outside the UK, dial your country's international calling code (usually 00), followed by 44 for the UK, followed by 29 for Cardiff, followed by the eight-digit number. To call Cardiff from another city in the UK, simply dial 029 and the eight-digit number.

TELEPHONING ABROAD

To phone abroad from anywhere in Wales, dial 00 followed by the country code and the local number. Country codes are listed in the phone directory and include: Australia 61; Canada 1; France 33; Germany 49; Ireland 353; New Zealand 64; USA 1.

ELECTRICITY

The electrical system in Wales is very reliable. It is 240 volts AC, 50 Hz. Square three-pin plugs are standard.

TRAVELLERS WITH DISABILITIES

Cardiff caters well for those with disabilities and has come a long way to becoming wheelchair-accessible. Many of the city's modern facilities, attractions and public buildings have been thoughtfully designed with disabled visitors in mind, often featuring wheelchair ramps, low-level lift buttons and accessible toilets.

As most of the major sights group in the compact and flat city centre, it is generally easy to get around. Running a frequent service from Cardiff Central Station to Cardiff Bay, the Bay Xpress bus is wheelchair-accessible. For more details, contact Cardiff Bus (see page 56).

Many of Cardiff's key venues and attractions offer reduced entry for disabled visitors. These include St David's Hall (see page 66) and the New Theatre (see page 96), with level floors and ramp access to the foyer. St Fagans National History Museum (see page 18), the National Museum Cardiff (see page 96) and Techniquest (see page 80) are also fully accessible. The Millennium Stadium (see page 66) has special viewing platforms holding up to 200 wheelchair users.

TOURIST INFORMATION

Cardiff Bay Visitor Centre This futuristic visitor centre is an attraction in its own right. The award-winning design built of steel and plywood is in the shape of a giant telescope. Step inside to take in a free exhibition and admire views of the bay. Tourist information and maps are available. ⓐ Harbour Drive ⓣ (029) 2046 3833 ⓦ www.cardiffharbour.com ⓒ 10.00–18.00 daily

Cardiff Tourist Information Centre In the heart of the capital, Cardiff's main tourist information centre provides information on local attractions, an accommodation booking service, Internet access and a left-luggage facility. ⓐ The Old Library, The Hayes ⓣ (029) 2087 3573 ⓦ www.visitcardiff.com ⓒ 09.30–17.30 Mon–Sat, 10.00–16.00 Sun

Well designed and illustrated, the *Visit Wales* site – ⓦ www.visitwales.com – is an invaluable tool for those travelling to Wales. The site lists tourist information centres across Wales.

BACKGROUND READING

Collected Poems, 1934–53 by Dylan Thomas. Brush up on your knowledge of the works of Wales's most famous poet.

Emergencies

The following are free nationwide emergency numbers:

Police, fire & ambulance ❶ 999

European emergency number ❶ 112 (This is the standard SOS number in all EU countries. The operator will connect you to the service you need.)

❶ When you dial the UK emergency services number 999:

- ask for the service you require
- give details of where you are, what the emergency is and the number of the phone you are using.

MEDICAL EMERGENCIES

Should you need emergency care, call 999 or 112 and ask for an ambulance. The Accident and Emergency Department is at the **University Hospital of Wales** in Heath Park (❶ (029) 2074 7747). Listings of doctors, some operating a 24-hour call-out service, can be found in the Yellow Pages directory.

Pharmacies usually open 08.30–18.00 Mon–Sat and 11.00–17.00 Sun. Dispensaries at major supermarkets often stay open later. For over-the-counter and prescription medications, **Boots the Chemist** has a number of branches across Cardiff, including the central branch on Queen Street (❶ (029) 2023 1291).

POLICE

Police officers in Wales wear dark blue uniforms and a conical helmet. The Cardiff Central Police Station in Cathays Park deals with enquiries. ❷ King Edward VII Av ❶ (029) 2022 2111

EMBASSIES & CONSULATES

Embassies and consulates dealing with passport and visa issues are based in London. Some of the major ones are:

Australian High Commission ⓐ Australia House, Strand
ⓣ (020) 7379 4334 ⓦ www.australia.org.uk

Canadian High Commission ⓐ MacDonald House, 1 Grosvenor Square ⓣ (020) 7258 6600 ⓦ www.canada.org.uk

Irish Embassy ⓐ 17 Grosvenor Place ⓣ (020) 7235 2171
ⓦ www.embassyofireland.co.uk

New Zealand High Commission ⓐ New Zealand House, 80 Haymarket
ⓣ (020) 7930 8422 ⓦ www.nzembassy.com

South African High Commission ⓐ South Africa House, Trafalgar Square ⓣ (020) 7451 7299 ⓦ www.southafricahouse.com

US Embassy ⓐ 24 Grosvenor Square ⓣ (020) 7499 9000
ⓦ www.usembassy.org.uk

🔺 *Mounted police outside Cardiff's lifeboat station*

INDEX

ACKNOWLEDGEMENTS

The publishers would like to thank the following individuals and organisations for supplying their copyright photographs for this book: The Photolibrary Wales/Alamy pages 5, 145; Catsper page 25; exioman page 9; Getty Images/Stephen Studd page 59; Meghan Hurst pages 45, 78, 127; Peter Morgan page 17; Gareth Peters/SXC.hu page 53; Robert and Tony page 155; Wendy Slattery page 140; Victoria Trott pages 21, 30, 56–7, 68, 103; Neil Setchfield all others.

Project editor: Rachel Norridge
Proofreaders: Caroline Hunt & Karolin Thomas
Layout: Donna Pedley

Send your thoughts to
books@thomascook.com

- Found a great bar, club, shop or must-see sight that we don't feature?

- Like to tip us off about any information that needs a little updating?

- Want to tell us what you love about this handy little guidebook and more importantly how we can make it even handier?

Then here's your chance to tell all! Send us ideas, discoveries and recommendations today and then look out for your valuable input in the next edition of this title.

Email the above address (stating the title) or write to: pocket guides Series Editor, Thomas Cook Publishing, PO Box 227, Coningsby Road, Peterborough PE3 8SB, UK.

WHAT'S IN YOUR GUIDEBOOK?

Independent authors Impartial up-to-date information from our travel experts who meticulously source local knowledge.

Experience Thomas Cook's 165 years in the travel industry and guidebook publishing enriches every word with expertise you can trust.

Travel know-how Thomas Cook has thousands of staff working around the globe, all living and breathing travel.

Editors Travel-publishing professionals, pulling everything together to craft a perfect blend of words, pictures, maps and design.

You, the traveller We deliver a practical, no-nonsense approach to information, geared to how you really use it.

Thomas Cook **pocket** guides

PARIS

Your travelling companion since 1873

Thomas
Cook